380

5220

(8) ✗

This book is to be returned on or before
the last date stamped below.

by the same author

plays

AFTER THEFALL
ALL MY SONS
THE AMERICAN CLOCK
THE ARCHBISHOP'S CEILING
THE CREATION OF THE WORLD, AND OTHER BUSINESS
THE CRUCIBLE
DEATH OF A SALESMAN
AN ENEMY OF THE PEOPLE (adapted from Ibsen)
INCIDENT AT VICHY
THE MAN WHO HAD ALL THE LUCK
A MEMORY OF TWO MONDAYS
THE PRICE
UP FROM PARADISE (musical)
A VIEW FROM THE BRIDGE

Screenplays

THE MISFITS
PLAYING FOR TIME

Prose fiction

FOCUS
I DON'T NEED YOU ANY MORE
JANE'S BLANKET (for children)

non-fiction

(with photographs by Inge Morath)
CHINESE ENCOUNTERS
IN RUSSIA
IN THE COUNTRY
'SALESMAN' IN BEIJING

Arthur Miller

Two-Way Mirror

A double-bill of
Elegy for a Lady
and
Some Kind of Love Story

With an Afterword by Christopher Bigsby

METHUEN · LONDON

Two-way Mirror first published in Great Britain in 1984 by
Methuen London Ltd, 11 New Fetter Lane, London EC4P 4EE.
Elegy for a Lady copyright © 1980, 1982, 1984 by Arthur Miller.
Some Kind of Love Story copyright © 1983, 1984 by Arthur Miller.
Front cover illustration, *Rind*, copyright © M.C. Escher Heirs,
c/o J.W. Vermeulen, Prilly, Switzerland.

Miller, Arthur
  Two-way mirror.
  I. Title   II. Miller, Arthur, Elegy for
  a lady.   III. Miller, Arthur, Some kind
  of love story
  812'.52   PS3525.I5156

  ISBN 0-413 55850-9
  ISBN 0-413-55860-6 Pbk

CAUTION

Printed in Great Britain by
Richard Clay (The Chaucer Press) Ltd,
Bungay, Suffolk

Some Kind of Love Story, in tandem with *Elegy for a Lady*, was presented by the Long Wharf Theater in New Haven, Connecticut, in November, 1982 under the omnibus title of *2 by A.M.* The production was directed by the author, with Christine Lahti and Charles Cioffi appearing in both plays. The sets were by Hugh Landwehr; costumes were by Bill Walker; and the lighting was by Ronald Wallace.

Author's Note

The stories and characters of this pair of plays are unrelated to one another but in different ways both works are passionate voyages through the masks of illusion to an ultimate reality. In *Some Kind of Love Story* it is social reality and the corruption of justice which a delusionary woman both conceals and unveils. The search in *Elegy for a Lady* is for the shape and meaning of a sexual relationship that is being brought to a close by a lover's probable death. In both the unreal is an agony to be striven against and, at the same time, accepted as life's condition.

A.M.

ELEGY FOR A LADY

It isn't always clear exactly where one stands in psychic space when grief passes up through the body into the mind. To be at once the observer and observed is a split awareness that most people know; but what of the grieved-for stranger, the other who is 'not-me'? – Doesn't it sometimes seem as though he or she is not merely outside oneself but also within and seeing outward through one's own eyes at the same time that he or she is being seen?

There is an anguish, based on desire impossible to realize, that is so unrequited, and therefore so intense, that it tends to fuse all people into one person in a so-to-speak spectral unity, a personification which seems to reflect and clarify these longings and may even reply to them when in the ordinary world of 'I' and 'You' they cannot even be spoken aloud. Nor is this really so strange when one recalls how much of each of us is imagined by the other, how we create one another even as we actually speak and actually touch.

A.M.

CAST

MAN
PROPRIETRESS

Music: it has a fine, distant fragility, a simple theme, repeated – like unresolved grief.

The MAN *appears in a single beam of light, facing the audience. He is hatless, dressed in a well-fitted overcoat and tweed suit.*

He stares as though lost in thought, slightly bent forward, perhaps to concentrate better. He is deep into himself, unaware for the moment of his surroundings.

Light rises behind him, gradually dawning across the stage, reveals aspects of what slowly turns out to be a boutique. The shop consists of its elements without the walls, the fragments seeming to be suspended in space.

A sweater is draped over a bust, a necklace on another bust, a garter on an upturned plastic thigh, a watch on an upturned arm, a knitted cap and muffler on a plastic head. Some of these stand on elements of the countershape, others seem to hang in air.

As the light rises to normal level the MAN *moves into the boutique. And now, among the displays a* WOMAN *is discovered standing, motionless, looking off at an angle in passive thought. She is wearing a white silk blouse and a light beige skirt and high heeled shoes. The* MAN *moves from object to object and pauses to look into the display case in the counter where jewellery is kept. As he nears her, he halts, staring into her profile. Music dies.*

MAN. Can you help me?

PROPRIETRESS (*turns now to look into his eyes*). Yes?

MAN. Do you have anything for a dying woman?

PROPRIETRESS (*startled, she waits a moment for him to continue and then looks about, trying to imagine*). Well, let me see . . .

He waits another instant, then resumes his search, examining a pair of gloves, a blouse.

May I ask you if . . . ?

She breaks off when he does not respond or turn to her. Finally, he does.

MAN. Excuse me?

PROPRIETRESS. I was just wondering if you meant that she was actually . . .

MAN. By the end of the month or so. Apparently.

PROPRIETRESS (*seeking hope*). . . . . But it isn't sure.

MAN. I think *she's* sure. But I haven't talked to any doctors or anything like that . . .

PROPRIETRESS. And it's . . ?

MAN (*cutting in*). So it seems, yes.

PROPRIETRESS (*helpless personal involvement*). Ah.

MAN (*forcing out the words*). . . . . I assume you were going to say cancer.

The PROPRIETRESS *nods with a slight inhale of air. Now she glances around at her stock with a new sense of urgency.*

I started to send flowers, but flowers seem so . . . funereal.

PROPRIETRESS. Not necessarily. Some spring flowers?

MAN. What's a spring flower? – daisies?

PROPRIETRESS. Or daffodils. There's a shop two blocks down – Faynton's.

MAN (*considers*). I passed there twice. But I couldn't decide if it should be a bunch of flowers or a plant.

PROPRIETRESS. Well, either would be . . .

MAN. Except that a bunch would fade, wouldn't they? – in a few days?

PROPRIETRESS. But a plant would last. For years, sometimes.

MAN. But there's a suggestion of irony in that. Isn't there?

PROPRIETRESS (*thinks*). Cut flowers, then.

MAN. They don't last at all, though, and she'd have to watch them withering away every morning . . .

PROPRIETRESS. Yes.

Slight pause. He resumes looking at things, handles a bracelet . . . half asking . . .

She is not an older woman.

MAN. She just turned thirty . . . a couple of months ago.

The PROPRIETRESS *inhales sharply.*

I've never really bought her anything. It struck me this afternoon. Nothing important.

PROPRIETRESS (*delicately*). You've known each other very . . .

MAN (*grieving*). That's always hard to remember exactly. I can never figure out whether we met two winters ago or three. (*A little laugh which she joins.*) – She never can either . . . but we've never been able to stay on the subject long enough . . . in fact, on any subject – Except one.

PROPRIETRESS *laughs softly and he joins her for an instant.*

I'm married.

PROPRIETRESS (*nods*). Yes.

MAN. And a lot older, of course.

PROPRIETRESS. Oh, Well that's not always a . . . (*She does not finish.*)

MAN. No, but it is in most cases. (*He glances around again.*) I tried to think of a book. But after all the reading I've done nothing occurs to me.

PROPRIETRESS. She is not religious.

MAN. No – Although we never talked about religion. I don't

know whether to try to concentrate her mind or distract it. Everything I can think to send her seems ironical; every book seems either too sad or too comical; I can't think of anything that won't increase the pain of it.

PROPRIETRESS. Perhaps you're being too tender. Nothing you could send would be as terrible as what she knows.

He considers this, nods slightly.

People do make a kind of peace with it.

MAN. No; I think in her case the alarm never stops ringing; living is all she ever thought about – She won't answer the phone anymore. She doesn't return my calls for days, a week sometimes. I think, well, maybe she wants me – you know – to disappear, but then she does call back and always makes an excuse for not having called earlier. And she seems so desperate for me to believe her that I forget my resentment and I try to offer to help again and she backs away again . . . and I end up not seeing her for weeks again. (*Slight pause.*) I even wonder sometimes if she's simply trying to tell me there's somebody else. I can't figure out her signal.

PROPRIETRESS. Yes. But then again it might simply be that she . . .

MAN. That's right . . .

PROPRIETRESS. . . . . Finds it unbearable to be cheated of someone she loves . . .

MAN. I'm so glad to hear you say that! – it's possible . . . (*With relief, deeper intimacy.*) Sometimes, you know, we're on the phone and suddenly she excuses herself – and there's silence for a whole minute or two. And then she comes back on with a fresh and forward-looking attitude and her voice clear. But a couple of times she's cut out a split second too late, and I hear the rush of sobbing before she can clap her hand to the receiver. And it just burns my mind – and then when she comes back on so optimistically I'm in a terrible conflict; should I insist on talking about the reality, or should I pretend to sort of swim along beside her?

PROPRIETRESS. She's in a hospital.

MAN. Not yet – Although, frankly, I'm not really sure. She's never home anymore. I know that. Unless she's stopped answering her phone altogether. – Even before this happened she would do that; but she's on the phone practically all day in her work so it is understandable. Not that I'm ruling out that she might have been staying elsewhere occasionally. – But of course I've no right to make any demands on her. Or even ask any questions. – What does this sound like to you?

PROPRIETRESS. It sounds like you'd simply like to thank her.

Music resumes behind his speech.

MAN (*with a slight surprise*). Say! That's exactly right, yes! . . . I'd simply like to thank her. I'm so glad it sounds that way.

PROPRIETRESS. Well . . . why not just *do* that?

MAN (*anguished*). But how can I without implying that she's coming to the end . . . ? (*He breaks off.*)

PROPRIETRESS. But she's *said* she's . . . ?

MAN. Not really in so many words; she just . . . as I told you . . . breaks up on the phone or . . .

Music dies away.

PROPRIETRESS (*with anguish now*). Then why are you so sure she's . . . ?

MAN. Because they're evidently operating on her in about ten days. And she won't tell me which hospital.

PROPRIETRESS. . . . When you say evidently . . .

MAN. Well. I know she's had this growth, and there was a pain for awhile – about last summer – but then it passed and she was told it was almost certainly benign. But . . .

(*He goes silent; stares at the* PROPRIETRESS.) Amazing.

PROPRIETRESS. Yes?

MAN. I've never mentioned her at all to anyone. And she has never let on about me. I know that . . . and we have close mutual friends who have no idea. And here I walk in and tell you everything, as though . . . (*From an engaging chuckle the breath seems to suddenly go out of him and he sits weakly on a stool, struggling against helplessness.*)
Music resumes.

PROPRIETRESS. Yes?

He makes an attempt to resume looking around the store but it fails.

When you passed here earlier today . . .

MAN (*with great relief*). Yes, that's right, I remember that! You saw me then . . .

PROPRIETRESS. You stared at the window for a very long time.

MAN. I was trying to think of something for her.
Music resumes.

PROPRIETRESS. Yes, I could see you imagining; it moved me deeply – for her sake.

MAN. It's amazing how absolutely nothing is right. I've been all over this part of town. But every single thing makes some kind of statement that is simply . . . not right.

PROPRIETRESS. I'm sure you're going to think of something.

MAN. I hope so!

PROPRIETRESS. Oh I'm sure!

MAN. It's partly, I think, that I don't know what I want to say because I'm not sure what I have a right to say – I mean someone my age ought to be past these feelings. – (*With sudden revulsion.*) I go on as though there's all the time in the world . . . ! (*He stands, quickened, looking at the goods again.*) That kerchief is beautiful.

PROPRIETRESS. It's silk. Paris. (*She unfurls it for him.*)

MAN. Lovely. How would you wear it?

PROPRIETRESS. Any way. Like this . . (*She drapes it over her shoulders.*)

MAN. Hm.

PROPRIETRESS. Or even as a bandanna. (*She wraps it over her hair.*)

MAN. But she wouldn't do that indoors.

PROPRIETRESS. Well . . . she *could*.

MAN. No. I'm afraid it could taunt her.

PROPRIETRESS (*putting it back on her shoulders*). Well, then – in bed, like this.

MAN (*tempted*). It is the right shade. – You have her colouring, you know; – I can't get over it, walking in off the street like this and blabbing away.

PROPRIETRESS. A thing like that builds up; you never know who you'll suddenly be telling it to.

MAN. Except that you have a look in your eye.

PROPRIETRESS (*smiling*). What kind of look?

MAN (*returns her smile*). You're seeing me. (*Of the scarf, definitely now.*) That isn't right. (*She slips it off. He moves, looking about.*) . . . I think it's also that you're just about her age.

PROPRIETRESS. Why would that matter?

MAN. Someone older usually forgets what thirty was really like.

PROPRIETRESS. But you remember?

MAN. I didn't used to – thirty is far back down the road for me; but when I'm with her it all flows back at the touch of her skin. I feel like a Hindu recalling a former life.

PROPRIETRESS. And what is thirty like?

Music resumes.

MAN. Thirty is an emergency. Thirty is the top of the ridge from where you can see down both sides – the sun and the shadow, your youth and your dying in the same glance. It's the last year to believe that your life can radically change anymore. And now she's caught on that ridge, unable to move. – God . . . (*A surge of anguish.*) . . . how *pleased* with herself she'd gotten lately! – her ambitions and plans really working out . . . (*With a half-proud, half-embarrassed grin.*) although tough too – she can snap your head back with a harsh truth, sometimes. But I don't mind, because all it is is her wide-open desire to live and win. (*He glances around at the objects.*). So it's hard to think of something that won't suggest the end of all that . . . and those eyes closing.

Music dies away.

PROPRIETRESS. I have a kind of warm negligee. That one up there.

MAN (*looks up, studies it for a moment*). But mightn't that look like something after you've had a baby?

PROPRIETRESS. Not necessarily.

MAN. Yes. Like when they stroll around the hospital corridors afterwards . . . If she's very sick she'd have to be in a hospital gown, wouldn't she?

PROPRIETRESS (*sharply, like a personal rebellion*). But *everybody* doesn't die of it! Not *every* case!

MAN (*explosively*). But she weeps on the phone! I *heard* it!

PROPRIETRESS (*a personal outcry*). Well the thought of disfigurement is terrible, isn't it? (*She turns away, pressing her abdomen. Pause.*) You ought to write, and simply thank her.

MAN (*asking . . .*). But that *has* to sound like a goodbye!

PROPRIETRESS. You sound as though you never had a single intimate talk!

MAN. Oh yes, but not about . . . negative things, somehow.

PROPRIETRESS. You met only for pleasure.

MAN. Yes. But it was also that we both knew there was

nowhere it could go. Not at my age. So things tend to float pretty much on the surface . . .

PROPRIETRESS (*smiling*). Still, the point does come . . .

MAN. Surprisingly, yes . . .

PROPRIETRESS. When it begins to be an effort to keep it un-committed . . .

MAN. Yes, there's a kind of contradiction . . .

PROPRIETRESS. – To care and simultaneously not-care . . .

MAN. You can't find a breakthrough – it's like a fish falling in love with the sun; once he breaks water he can't breathe! – So maybe the whole thing really doesn't amount to anything very much. (*Pause.*)

PROPRIETRESS (*she re-folds a sweater he had opened up*). But you don't always look like this, do you?

MAN. How?

PROPRIETRESS. In pain.

MAN. I guess I'm still unable to understand what she means to me. – I've never felt this way about a death. Even my mother's and father's . . . there has always been some un-welcome, tiny feeling of release; an obligation removed. But in her case, I feel I'm being pulled under myself and suffocated.

The PROPRIETRESS *takes a deeper breath of air and runs a hand down her neck.*

What else do you have that might . . . ? (*He halts as he starts once again to look around at the merchandise.*) . . . Wait! I know – a bed jacket! That's the kind of neutral – healthy people wear them too!

PROPRIETRESS. I haven't any.

MAN. Nothing at all?

PROPRIETRESS. You might try the department stores.

MAN (*greatly relieved*). I will. I think that's what I want. A bed jacket doesn't necessarily *say* anything, you see?

PROPRIETRESS. That's true, there is something non-committal about a bed jacket. Try Saks.

MAN. Yes. Thanks very much. – I never dreamed I'd have such a conversation! (*He starts to button up. With embarrassment . . .*) It really amazes me . . . coming in here like this . . .

PROPRIETRESS. I have an electric kettle if you'd care for a cup of tea.

MAN. . . . Thanks, I wouldn't mind, thanks very much . . . I simply can't get over it, . . . I had no idea all this was in me.

She goes behind the counter, throws a switch; he sits at the counter again.

Are you the owner here? (*He opens his coat again.*)

PROPRIETRESS (*nods, affirmatively, then . . .*). You know, it may be a case of a woman who's simply terrified of an operation, that's all. – I'm that way.

MAN (*thinks, trying to visualise – then . . .*). No, I think it would take a lot more to panic her like this. She's not an hysterical person, except once a month for a few hours, maybe.

PROPRIETRESS. She tends to objectify her situation.

MAN. That's it.

PROPRIETRESS. Sees herself.

MAN. Yes.

PROPRIETRESS. From a distance.

MAN. Yes, she has guts; really cool nerve right up to the moment she flies to pieces.

PROPRIETRESS. She's had to control because she's alone.

MAN. Yes; so something like this must be like opening a shower curtain and a wild animal jumps out.

PROPRIETRESS. She was never married.

MAN. Never. (*He begins to stare off and smile.*)

PROPRIETRESS. Something about her couldn't be. – Unless

to you?

MAN (*joyfully*). She has a marvellous, throaty, almost vulgar laugh; it can bend her forward and she even slaps her thigh like a hick comedian . . .

The PROPRIETRESS *begins laughing.*

And gets so helpless she hangs on my arm and nearly pulls me down to the sidewalk.

The PROPRIETRESS *laughs more deeply.*

One time at one of those very tiny café tables we both exploded laughing at the same instant, and our heads shot forward just as the waiter was lowering my omelette between us . . .

She bursts out laughing and slaps her thigh. Music: sharply. He sees this and his smile remains. The tea kettle whistles behind the counter.

PROPRIETRESS. Milk or lemon?

He watches her a moment, smiling.

Lemon?

MAN. Lemon, yes.

(*She goes and pours tea. The* MAN, *with a new anticipatory excitement.*) You're not busy?

Music dies away.

PROPRIETRESS. After Christmas it all dies for a few days. (*She hands him a cup.*)

MAN. It's more like somebody's home in here.

PROPRIETRESS. I try to sell only what I'd conceivably want for myself, yes.

MAN. You're successful.

PROPRIETRESS. In a way. (*Confusing.*) . . . I am, I guess. – Very, in fact.

MAN. But a baby would be better.

PROPRIETRESS (*a flash of resentment, but then truth*). Sometimes. (*She hesitates.*) Often, actually. (*She looks around at the shop.*) It's all simply numbers, figures. Something appalling about business, something totally pointless – like emptying a pail and filling it again every day. – Why? – Do I look unhappy?

MAN. You look like you'd found yourself . . . for the fiftieth time and would love to throw yourself away again.

PROPRIETRESS. You try to avoid hurting people.

MAN. Yes, but it can't be helped sometimes. I've done it.

PROPRIETRESS. No wonder she loves you.

MAN. I'm not so sure. I really don't know anymore.

PROPRIETRESS. Oh, it must be true.

MAN. Why?

PROPRIETRESS. It would be so easy.

MAN. But I'm so old.

PROPRIETRESS. No.

MAN. I'm not sure I want her to. I warned her not to, soon after we started. I said there was no future in it. I said that these things are usually a case of loving yourself and wanting someone else to confirm it, that's all. I said all the blunt and ugly things I could think of.

PROPRIETRESS. And it didn't matter at all. (*Slight pause.*)

MAN. It didn't?

PROPRIETRESS (*with a hard truthfulness*). Of course it mattered – what you said made her stamp on her feelings, and hold part of herself in reserve. It even humiliated her a little.

MAN (*in defence*). But her independence means more to her than any relationship, I think.

PROPRIETRESS. How do you know? – You were the one who ordered her not to love you . . .

MAN. Yes. (*Evading her eyes.*) But there's no tragic error, necessarily – I don't think she wanted to love anyone. In fact, I don't think either of us said or did anything we badly regret – it's Nature that made the mistake; that I should be so much older, and so perfectly healthy and she so young and sick.

PROPRIETRESS (*unnerved, an outburst*). Why do you go on assuming it has to be the end!

He looks at her with surprise.

Thousands of people survive these things. And why couldn't you ask her what exactly it was?

MAN. I couldn't bear to make her say it.

PROPRIETRESS. Then all she's actually said was that an operation .. ?

MAN. No. Just that the 28th of the month was a big day.

PROPRIETRESS (*almost victoriously*). Well that could mean almost anything.

MAN (*in anguish*). Then why doesn't she let me come and see her!

PROPRIETRESS (*frantically*). Because she doesn't want to load her troubles onto you!

MAN. I've thought of that.

PROPRIETRESS. Of course. It's a matter of pride. Even before this happened, she never encouraged you to just drop in, for instance – did she?

MAN. Oh no. On the contrary.

PROPRIETRESS. Of course not! She wanted her hair to be done and be dressed in something you'd like her in . . .

MAN. Oh, insisted on that, yes.

PROPRIETRESS. Then you can hardly expect her to invite you to see her in hospital! (*Slight pause.*)

MAN. Then it *is* pretty superficial, isn't it?

PROPRIETRESS. Why! – it could be the most important thing in her entire life.

MAN (*pause. Shakes his head*). No. Important – but not the most important. Because neither of us have burned our bridges. As how could we? – If only because of my age?

PROPRIETRESS. Why do you go on about your age? That's only an excuse to escape with.

MAN (*smiles*). But it's the only one I've got, dear. – But whatever age I was, she wouldn't be good to be married to.

PROPRIETRESS (*hurt, almost alarmed*). How can you say that!

MAN. What's wrong in saying it? She's still ambitious for herself, she still needs risks, accomplishments, new expectations; she needs the dangerous mountains not marriage in the valley – marriage would leave her restless, it would never last. (*Pause.*)

PROPRIETRESS (*dryly*). Well, then . . . you were both satisfied . . .

(*As he turns to her, surprised.*) . . . with what you had.

MAN. That's a surprise – I never thought of that. Yes; very nearly. (*He thinks further.*) Almost. Yes. (*Slight pause.*) That's a shock, now.

PROPRIETRESS. To realise that you were almost perfectly happy.

MAN. Almost – You see, there was always – of necessity – something so tentative about it and uncertain, that I never thought of it as perfect, but it was – a perfect chaos. Amazing.

PROPRIETRESS. And your wife?

MAN (*slight pause*). My wife is who I should be married to. We've always helped one another. I'll always be grateful for having her. Especially her kindness.

PROPRIETRESS. She's not ambitious.

MAN. Yes; within bounds. We're partners in a business – advisory service for town planners. She's tremendously competent; I oversee; do less and less, though.

PROPRIETRESS. Why? Isn't it important?

MAN. Certainly is – we've changed whole countrysides for the next hundred years.

PROPRIETRESS. Then why do less and less?

MAN. I won't be here in a hundred years. – That struck me

powerfully one morning. (*Pause.*)

PROPRIETRESS. So – all in all – you will survive this.

MAN (*catching the implied rebuke*). That's right. And in a while, whole days will go by when her anguish barely crosses my mind; and then weeks, and then months, I imagine. (*Slight pause.*) And as I say this, I know that at this very moment she may well be keeping herself hidden from me so as not to wound me with her dying.

PROPRIETRESS. Or wound herself.

He looks at her questioningly.

If she doesn't have to look at what she's lost she loses less. – But I don't believe it's as bad as you make it. She's only keeping you away so that you won't see her so frightened of the knife. She has sense.

MAN. But why! – I would try to comfort her!

PROPRIETRESS (*strongly, angrily protesting*). But she doesn't want comfort, she wants her power back! You came to her for happiness, not some torn flesh bleeding on the sheets! She knows how long pity lasts! (*Slight pause.*)

MAN. Then what are you saying? – That there is really no gift I can give her at all? – Is that what you say?

PROPRIETRESS, *silent, lowers her eyes.*

There is really nothing between us, is there – nothing but an . . . uncommitment? (*He grins.*) Maybe that's why it's so hard to think of something to give her . . . She asked me once – as we were getting up at the end of an evening – she said, 'Can you remember all the women you've had?' Because she couldn't remember all the men, she said.

PROPRIETRESS. And did you believe her?

MAN. No. I thought she was merely reassuring me of her in-difference – that she'd never become demanding. It chilled me up the spine.

PROPRIETRESS. Really! Why?

MAN. Why say such a thing unless she had a terrific urge to

hold onto me?

PROPRIETRESS. But now you've changed your mind . . .

He turns to her surprised.

MAN. No, I kind of think now she was telling the truth. I think there is some flow of indifference in her, cold and remote, like water flowing in a cave. As there is in me. (*Slight pause.*) I feel you're condemning me now.

PROPRIETRESS. I never condemn anyone; you know that. I can't.

MAN. I know. But still, deep, deep down . . .

PROPRIETRESS. No. I'm helpless not to forgive everything, finally.

MAN. That's your glory, but in some deepest part of you there has to be some touch of contempt . . .

PROPRIETRESS. What are you saying? – You carefully offered only your friendship, didn't you?

MAN. But what more could I offer!

PROPRIETRESS. Then you can't expect what you would have had if you'd committed yourself, can you.

MAN. What I would have had . . ?

Music resumes.

PROPRIETRESS. Yes! – To be clung to now, to be worn out with weeping, to be staggered with your new loneliness, to be clarified with grief, washed with it, cleansed by a whole sorrow. A lover has to earn that satisfaction. If you couldn't bring yourself to share her life, you can't expect to share her dying. Is that what you'd like?

MAN. I would like to understand what I was to her.

PROPRIETRESS (*protesting*). You were her friend!

MAN (*shakes his head*). There is no such thing. No! No! No! What is a friend who only wants the good news and the bright side? I love her. But I am forbidden to by my commitments, by my age, by my aching joints – great God almighty, I'm sleepy by half-past nine! The whole thing is ludicrous, what could she have seen in me? I can't bear the sight of my face in the mirror – I'm shaving my father every morning!

PROPRIETRESS. Then why not believe her – you were . . . simply one of her friends.

Music dies away.

MAN (*pause*). One of her . . . friends. Yes. – I'll have to try to accept that. (*Slight pause.*) But why doesn't it empty me? Why am I still filled like this? What should I do that I haven't done – or say that I haven't said to make some breakthrough? (*Weeping.*) My God, what am I saying! (*Imploring.*) You know. Tell me!

PROPRIETRESS. Perhaps . . . that it's perfect, just as it is? *He slowly turns from her, absorbing her voice.*

That it is all that it could ever have become? (*Pause.*)

MAN. You feel that? – You believe that?

PROPRIETRESS. Yes.

MAN. . . . That we are as close now as we ever can come?

PROPRIETRESS. Yes. – But she believes she's going to make it, she knows she'll live.

MAN. So she's simply . . . momentarily afraid.

PROPRIETRESS. Oh, terribly, yes.

MAN (*with gathering hope*). That's possible; and it's true that she'd never wish to be seen that scared, especially by me. She has contempt for cowardice, she rises to any show of bravery – any! I think you're possibly right; she'll want to see me when she's made it! When she's a winner again!

PROPRIETRESS. I'm sure of it.

MAN. On the other hand . . . (*He breaks off suddenly; as though a hollowness opens beneath him his face goes expressionless.*) . . . it's also possible, isn't it . . . that . . .

PROPRIETRESS (*cutting him off, with dread*). Why go further? You'll know everything soon.

MAN. Not if I can't see her. She won't say the name of the

hospital.

PROPRIETRESS (*she touches his hand*). But why go further?

MAN. But if she . . . dies?

PROPRIETRESS. She doesn't expect to.

MAN (*with confidence, an awareness*). Or she does expect to. *And he turns to her; she is filled with love and anguish; he speaks directly to her, gripping her hand in his.*

Either way, my being with her now . . . would only deepen it between us when it should not be deepened, because very soon now I will be far too old. If she makes it . . . it would not be good for us – to have shared such agony. It won't cure age, nothing will – *That's* it.

She offers her lips, he kisses her.

It's that she doesn't want it spoiled you see, by deepening.

PROPRIETRESS (*she embraces him, her body pressed to his, an immense longing in it and a sense of a last embrace*). She wants to make it stay exactly as it is . . . forever. (*She presses his face to hers, they kiss.*) How gently! (*He kisses her again. With a near cry of farewell . . .*) Oh how gently! (*He slips from her embrace; a new thought as he looks around the shop. Filled, directed by his grief.*)

MAN. Then what I ought to send her is something she could definitely keep for a long time. (*He is quickened as he looks about, as though he almost knows beforehand what to seek. He moves more quickly from object to object, and at a tray of costume jewellery he halts, draws out a watch on a gold chain.*) Does this work? (*He winds it.*)

PROPRIETRESS. Oh yes, it's exact. It's an antique.

MAN (*puts the watch to his ear, then couches it in his hand, hefts it, then hangs it from the neck of the* PROPRIETRESS *and stands back to look at it on her.*) Yes, it's beautiful.

PROPRIETRESS. I know.

He starts to take out his wallet . . .

Take it.

Music resumes but more rapidly now.

She takes it off her neck and holds it out, hanging it before him; he puts back his wallet. The implication freezes him.

Go ahead – it's just the right thing; it will tell her to be brave each time she looks at it.

He takes the watch and chain and looks at them in his hand.

You never said her name. (*She starts to smile.*)

MAN (*starting to smile*). You never said yours. (*Slight pause.*) Thank you. Thank you . . . very much.

On each of their faces a grin spreads – of deep familiarity. The light begins to lower; with the smile still on his face he moves away from the setting until he is facing front, staring. The woman and the boutique go dark, vanishing. He strolls away, alone..

Music dies away.

SOME KIND OF LOVE STORY

CAST

ANGELA
TOM O'TOOLE

The action takes place in ANGELA's bedroom, in an American city. Time: the present.

A bed in a darkened room. A window. The headboard of the bed is white plastic tufting with gold trim, Grand Rapids Baroque. A door Upstage to the bathroom. Another at Right to the living-room. Skirts, bras, shoes, articles of clothing dropped everywhere. ANGELA *is barely visible sitting up on the bed. The Right door opens.*

TOM O'TOOLE *sticks his head in.*

TOM. Are we decent?

ANGELA. Christ's sake, close the door.

TOM. Lemme get in first! (*He shuts the door behind him, pushes back his narrow brimmed hat, unbuttons his raincoat, and is forced to peer through the murky air to see her face.*) Well! – You're sounding nice and spunky, how's it goin' tonight?

ANGELA. Philly out there?

TOM. In the kitchenette, lip-readin' his racin' form.

ANGELA. Say anything to you?

TOM. Nooo. Just laid one of his outraged-husband looks on me again. What do you say I buy you a spaghetti? – Come on.

ANGELA. You can turn on the light. And lock the door, will you?

TOM. What's with the rollers? You going out?

She undoes a roller now that her attention has been drawn to it. He locks the door and switches a lamp on. She is sitting up in bed, permed hair, black slip, pink wrapper. She lights a cigarette.

Jeeze, you really are swollen. You want ice?

ANGELA (*works her jaw, touching it*). It's going down.

TOM (*sitting on a stool beside the bed*). Hope you don't mind, darlin', but a man who takes his fists to his wife ought to be strung up by his testicles one at a time.

ANGELA (*a preoccupied air*). Nobody's perfect. He can't help himself, he's immature.

TOM. Well, maybe I'll understand it sometime – It's amazing, I always leave here with more questions than I came in with.

ANGELA. He's still the father of my daughter. (*She gets off the bed, tidies up the room a bit.*) By the way, she called me from L.A. She's going to apply to the University of California, being she's so fantastic in basketball.

TOM (*dropping into a chair, hat and coat still on*). Well, that'd be nice, wouldn't it? You're lucky to have a kid these days who loves you.

ANGELA. Don't yours?

TOM. Yeah, but they're exceptional. Anyway, I'm unusually loveable. (*He guffaws.*)

ANGELA. What're you laughing at? – It's true. (*Sadly.*) You're probably the most loveable man I've ever met.

TOM (*to get down to business*). You caught me climbin' into bed when you called.

ANGELA. I appreciate you coming, Tom – this had to be my worst day yet. (*She moves to a window to look into the back-yard.*)

TOM. No kiddin'. On the phone you sounded like you seen a ghost.

ANGELA (*a wan smile*). You ever going to love me again?

TOM. Always will, honey – in spirit.

The answer turns her sadder; she restlessly walks in sighing frustration.

I explained it, Ange–

ANGELA. What'd you explain?

TOM. You are part of the case in a certain way; and I can't be concentrating on this case and banging you at the same time. It's all wrong. I'm being as straight as I can with you. – What happened today?

ANGELA. I don't know – it just hit me again like a ton of bricks that Felix is still sitting in that cell.

TOM. That's right; it'll be five years October.

ANGELA. You tend to get used to it after so long but today I simply . . . I couldn't stand it all over again.

TOM. I can't stand it *every* day.

ANGELA (*as though reawakened to his value*). You're a wonderful man, Tom. You're really one of a kind.

TOM. Personally, I wouldn't mind sharin' the distinction, but I don't see too many volunteers on *this* case.

ANGELA (*she looks off, shaking her head with wonder at his character*). Be proud of yourself – I mean with all the great people in this state, the colleges, the churches, the newspapers, and nobody lifts a finger except you . . . I simply can't believe he's still in there!

TOM (*sensing attenuation*). What'd you want to see me about, Ange?

ANGELA (*glances at him, then gets up again, moves*). I'm really teetering. My skin is so tight I could scream.

TOM. What happened today?

ANGELA. God how I love to see you sitting here and the sound of your voice . . . (*At the window.*) . . . Is that drizzle comin' down again?

TOM. But it's kind of warm out; you want to try to walk it off? Come on, I'll take you to the boardwalk, buy you a chowder.

ANGELA (*moves restlessly*). God, how I hate this climate.

TOM. I thought it reminded you of Sweden.

ANGELA. I'm a Finn, not a Swede; I said it was *like* Finland

– Not that I was ever *in* Finland.

TOM (*a grin*). So how's my standing tonight?

ANGELA. You're always in my top three; you know that.

TOM (*wryly*). Not always, Ange – last time I was practically wiped off the scoreboard.

ANGELA (*genuinely surprised*). What are you talking about?

TOM. You ordered me never to show my face again, don't you remember?

ANGELA (*vaguely recalling a probability*). Well, you were probably pressuring me, that's all; I will not submit to pressure . . .

TOM. Well, *you* called *me* tonight, kid. So what's it about?

ANGELA. What the hell is this goddam rush, suddenly?

TOM (*laughs*). Rush! You have any idea how long we've been bullshitting around together about this case? It's damn near five years!

ANGELA. And every single thing you know about it came from me and don't you forget it either.

TOM. Well . . . not everything . . .

ANGELA (*a shot of angry indignation*). *Everything!*

TOM (*a sigh*). Well, all right. – But I'm still nowhere.

ANGELA. This is a whole new side of you, isn't it?

TOM (*sensing her fear – gently*). Baby Doll, the last time on Thursday I spent seven-and-one-half hours in this room with you . . .

ANGELA. It was nowhere *near* seven and . . .

TOM (*suppressing explosion*). Until two-thirty a.m. when you give me such a kick in the balls that if it'd landed I'd have gone into orbit. So we can call tonight a strictly professional visit to hear whatever you got to say about the case of Felix Epstein . . . and *nothing else*. – Now what'd you want to tell me?

ANGELA (*dismissing him*). Well, I can't talk to you in a mechanical atmosphere.

TOM (*gets up*). Then goodnight and happy dreams.

ANGELA. What are you doing?

TOM (*a strained laugh*). Gettin' back into my pyjamas! – I have driven here through half an hour of fog and rain!

ANGELA (*open helplessness*). I'm desperate to talk to you! Why don't you give me a chance to open my mouth? (*Turning her back on him, moving . . .*) I mean, shit, if you want a mechanical conversation go see your friendly Ford dealer.

TOM. I'll tell you something, Angela – you're just lucky I'm still in love with you.

ANGELA (*she smiles now, tragically*). You wouldn't be kidding about that if I wasn't a sick woman – I'd have walked you off into the sunset five years ago and don't think I couldn't have done it.

TOM. My wife thinks you could still do it.

ANGELA. Go on, she knows why you see me nowadays.

TOM. Maybe that's why she's talkin' separation.

ANGELA. One of the nicest things about you, Tom, is that you're so obvious when you're full of shit.

TOM. She thinks we're still making it, Angela.

ANGELA (*breaks into a smile, warm and pleasured, gets up and comes to him, takes off his hat and kisses the top of his head*). Honestly?

TOM. I mean it. From the way I talk about you she says she can tell.

ANGELA (*sliding her hand towards his crotch*). Well as long as she believes it, why don't we again?

TOM (*grasping her wrists*). Y'know . . . I had to give up the booze twenty years ago, and then the cigarettes because the doctor told me I have the make-up of an addict. If I went into you again I'd never come out the rest of my life.

ANGELA (*seizing the respite*). Were you ever really in love, Tom?

TOM (*hesitates, then nods*). Once.

ANGELA. I don't mean as a kid . . .

TOM. No, I was about twenty-five.

ANGELA. What happened to her?

TOM (*hesitates, then grins in embarrassment*). My mother didn't approve.

ANGELA. Why not, she wasn't Catholic?

TOM. She was Catholic.

ANGELA (*a wide grin*). A tramp?

TOM. No! But she knew I'd stayed over with her a couple of times. And we were a strict family, see.

ANGELA. You've still got a lot of priest in you, Tom – I love that about you.

TOM. You do? I don't. Leaving that woman was the biggest mistake I ever made. In fact, five or six years later, I was already married but I went back looking for her – I was ready to leave my wife – But she was gone, nobody knew where.

ANGELA (*romantically*). And you really still think of her?

TOM. More now than ever. In that respect I lived the wrong life.

ANGELA (*she is staring at him, an open expression on her face. On her knees beside his chair she rests her head on his shoulder*). Life is so wrong – a man like you ought to be happy all day and all night long.

ANGELA *sings 'When Irish Eyes Are Smiling'. He corrects a couple of mistakes.*

TOM (*intimately, breaking into the song*). Tell me the truth, Angela – are you ever going to unload what you know about the Epstein case?

ANGELA (*slight pause. She is deeply fearful, but taking pleasure, too, in his concern*). I'm so worried about myself, Tom. I think I did some kind of a number today, right in the middle of Crowley Square.

TOM (*grinning*). I know when you're changing the subject, kid.

ANGELA (*angered*). It scared me to death, for Christ's sake! – I'm still shaking!

TOM. What happened?

ANGELA (*a moment to let her indignation sink in*). I'm walking along past the piano store – Ramsey's?

TOM. And?

ANGELA. All I remember next is I'm sitting on the fender of a parked car with a whole crowd of people around me. A couple of young guys were sniggering – like I'd done something indecent or something – they had that look, y'know? (*A deepening of overtly fearful breathing.*) I've really got to get to a doctor, Tom.

TOM. Okay.

ANGELA. I go blotto for longer and longer stretches, I think. Sometimes I get the feeling that I don't know where the hell I been all day, or what I said, or to who I said it.

TOM. You want me to arrange a psychiatrist?

ANGELA. With what, though?

TOM. Maybe I can get one on the tab. You want one?

ANGELA (*a sigh*). I don't know, everyone I ever went to ends up trying to get into my pants. Anyway, I know what they'll tell me – I'm a schizophrenic. So what else is new? Why are you so resentful tonight?

TOM. Honey, it's the same schizophrenia conversation we had fifteen different times, and it's eleven p.m.

ANGELA. What I am trying to tell you is that my heart is hanging by a thread, I haven't got very long. Or is that important?

TOM. Then why don't you tell me what you know before it's too late? The man is still innocent and he's still dying by inches in prison; his wife is a walking wreck, her parents are ready for the morgue, and you have the key to this case, Angela – I know it as sure as I know my name – and you jerk me around month after month, a crumb here and a crumb there. . . . I'm so exhausted I can't sleep! – And now you take to dragging me out of bed every other night to chat me up? (*She covers her eyes suddenly.*) Maybe it'd be good if you saw Felix again – you haven't been up there in a year, I could drive you . . .

ANGELA (*this touched a nerve*). I don't want to see him.

TOM (*surprised*). You mean *never*?

ANGELA. I've done more for Felix Epstein than you or anybody. I led the fight all by myself, for Christ's sake!

TOM. Honey, I don't know too much about the head, but as one ex-Catholic to another . . .

ANGELA. I'm not 'ex'.

TOM. Well, semi-ex. What's eatin' you alive is not schizophrenia, kid, it's your conscience.

ANGELA (*with shaky sarcasm*). You been talking to your friendly Jewish psychiatrist again, I see.

TOM. He's not my psychiatrist, he's interested in the case.

ANGELA. Well if that's what he thinks I'm up to, you can tell him from me he's full of shit.

TOM. I'll send him an immediate wire. (*He makes to leave.*) I'm really beat . . .

ANGELA (*instantly stopping him*). Wait, I just want you to tell me one thing. Sit down a second. Don't be this way – (*They sit.*) Why are you on this case?

TOM (*shocked – a near screech*). *What*!!

ANGELA (*sharply*). Well, don't be mad, I'm trying to tune myself! They're yelling tonight.

TOM (*quieting*). You're hearing them now? (*She nods. He is awkward making this absurdly obvious explanation.*) Well, the Epsteins hired me to clear Felix, they paid me five thousand dollars. – How do you pop a question like that after all these years?

ANGELA. Simply that if I told you what I know . . . (*A near stutter.*) . . . what, what . . . when would I ever see you again – on television? The great detective who broke the Epstein case . . . ?

TOM. In other words you backed me out of my pyjamas to be the Ladies Home Companion again.

He starts angrily for the door, but she flies to him in what he sees is a genuine terror.

ANGELA. No! Tom, you can't go! Oh, God you can't leave me tonight . . . Tom, Tom, please, you mustn't . . . ! Not tonight! (*She has a grip on him and pulls him back to the chair, forcing him into it.*) . . . you got to stay . . . just a little while . . .

TOM. God Almighty, what has got you so scared?

Trembling, she returns to sit on the bed.

ANGELA. Let's just be peaceful for a while, okay? (*Making conversation.*) What . . . what's it like out?

TOM (*reaching into his side pocket, ignoring her question*). You know what I done?

ANGELA (*grateful for the diversion, smiles, mimicking*). What'd you done?

TOM. Finally bought myself a notebook . . . (*He takes out a black looseleaf notebook.*) This is amazing – you askin' me why I'm in the case – because I sat down after lunch and started making a resume of the case right from day one, and it suddenly jumped off the page at me. (*A grin.*) That I had no explanation why *you* were involved in this case in the first place. At all and whatsoever. That funny?

ANGELA. Why shouldn't I be?

TOM. But why should you be, honey? (*A grinding laugh.*) You never knew Felix before his arrest; *or* the parents. And there you were in the courtroom every single day of the trial, and startin' up a defence committee yet! – I'd just always taken it for granted that you belonged there!

ANGELA. Why not! – I had nothing to do in the daytime and I kept reading about the case in the papers so I came to see.

He glances up at her with a look of open scepticism.

Why don't you come out with it?

She is almost visibly swept by a furiously pleasurable release, a sense of her real self; she stands, throwing out one hip, arms akimbo, mouth distorted into a tough sneer and her voice goes rough as gravel.

What you mean is how does a fuckin' whore come off attending a . . .

TOM. Now wait, I did not call you a . . .

ANGELA. Go on, you're full of shit – you know I've been a hooker!

TOM. I never said . . .

ANGELA. Oh, fuck off, will ya! You've snooped around, say it! – I've hooked the Holiday Inn, Travelodge . . .

TOM. Cut it out, Angela.

ANGELA. . . . Howard Johnson's, Ramada Inn . . . I've spread my ass on every barstool in this misbegotten, reamedout village . . . why don't you say it?

TOM (*helplessly*). I did not mean that you . . .

ANGELA. Say it! – How does a common slut *presume* . . .

TOM (*erupting*). I did not cast any such aspersion, Angela . . . !

ANGELA (*bending over to shout*). . . . *Presume* to involve herself in high class causes!

TOM (*mystified and alarmed*). What *is* this?

ANGELA (*she seems actually blind, enraged*). Well, you can get your filthy parish mind off my ass, you Irish mutt!

TOM (*suddenly aware, stepping back from her*). . . . Oh, God, is this a number?

ANGELA (*cupping her breasts to thrust them forward, mimics him*). 'Oh, God!' Grab onto this you jerked-off choir boy

. . . come on, get your finger out of your yum-yum and try some of this!

TOM (*holding his head*). Holy God.

ANGELA. Go on, you don't kid me . . . (*Turning and trying to force his hand onto her buttocks.*) Grab hold, you fucking milk-face, you think you're better than anybody else?

TOM. Angela, Jesus . . . !

(*A struggle; he forces her onto the bed. She screams and tries to fight him off, loses her wind, and gasping, as he stands up, watching him . . . pushing his hands off.*)

ANGELA. Well, if you can't get it up get goin'. I've got a line into the street tonight. Tip the hatcheck girl – if you can part with a dollar. And the name is Leontine in case you want to ask for me next time. (*She has gradually lost an inner pressure and seems to fall asleep.* O'TOOLE *goes and bends over her, moved and mystified. He draws a blanket over her. Then he straightens up and peers into the air, goes to the phone and dials.*)

TOM (*sotto voce, with glances toward the bed*). Hello? That you Mrs Levy? Tom O'Toole here. (*Charmingly.*) You sounded like your daughter! – Oh, pretty fair, thanks; the doctor said I could call anytime and I . . . – Oh, thanks very much, I'm really sorry for the hour. – Really! – I never thought you people watched TV! Thanks. (*He waits, glances over to* ANGELA, *then stares front with a certain eagerness.*) Hey, Josh, how are ya! – (*Nods.*) I'm there now but I might have to hang up, she just blew herself out. – Yeah, just like I described to you. Listen, I just got an idea. – Bad, very bad; really, really off the wall tonight, maybe the worst yet; in fact she just did a new one on me that I never saw before; Leontine, a real house whore. Horrendous vulgarity; you know, right off the knuckles. Listen, I gotta be quick – something just struck me; could a person have delusions, but like inside the delusion is the facts? What I'm trying to say, Josh . . . is that I got a gut feeling tonight that *somebody might really be threatening her life.* – Hell, I don't *know* why, but it's very hard to watch her and believe that she's stoking the whole thing up from inside, you see? I mean if they really want to get rid of her it verifies a lot of what she's been saying, you see? – Right! 'Cause I can't help it, Josh. I still believe that the key to this case is under that pantyhose. (*Listens avidly.*) Oh, she's definitely had Mob connections, that's objective; Johnny Gates kept her something like two years. – Gates? He's the head honcho. Numero Uno. But I checked the apartment house myself and she used to live there, no questions about it. – Listen, I might've given you the wrong idea – everything factual she's told me has stacked up with my own information. (*He laughs.*). No no, I've got great respect for fantasy; look, I was six years on the New York Vice Squad, how fantastic can you get? – Yes, please, go ahead. (*He listens.*) In what sense, my relation? (*Blushingly.*) Well, you must've guessed, didn't you? We rolled around together last spring but I finally decided to go back to the *status quo ante.* – Well, I got some bad feelings; started to wonder if they had her back working for them again. – Ya, basically prostitution. In fact, I think hubby may be the pimp, he's been punching her around again lately and that's typical pimp relationship. – Ya, but I thought she'd gotten out of that a long time ago. Even on the Vice Squad as a young guy I never touched them; I don't even like public swimming pools! (*Sees* ANGELA *moving.*) She's moving around . . . – I read you . . . but see she's got some terrific perceptions, sees right through to your spinal cord . . . she can be terrific company, wonderful sense of humour . . . I mean she's not *always crazy.* – But I think I'm *being* objective; maybe sometimes you've got to go to crazy people for the facts, though . . . maybe facts are what's making them crazy unless I'm bananas too, by this time. (*She is sitting up, looking around.*) Gotta go. (*He hangs up.*) How you doin', dear? (*She turns to him, sharp surprise.*) . . . I been here a few minutes.

ANGELA. How long you been here?

TOM. Few minutes.

ANGELA. Was that Philly knocking?

TOM. I didn't hear any knocking, you must've been dreaming.

ANGELA (*slight pause – she stares at the door*). Would you go and see if they're still out there?

TOM. Who's that, dear?

ANGELA. The cops.

TOM. What cops you mean?

ANGELA. The cruiser. They've been parking a cruiser on the street almost all the time. Didn't you see it when you came?

TOM. . . . Well, no, I didn't notice.

ANGELA. Well, go and take a look out front. Go ahead.

TOM (*suspending disbelief, hoping it is true.*) Okay. (*He unlocks the door, exits, as . . .*)

ANGELA. Look out the bay window – usually towards Rodman Street.

She turns front, fear in her face, an attempt at concentration . . . he re-enters, shuts the door and walks into the room. She rather quickly goes and locks the door, always glancing at him for his report.

TOM. Don't see any cruiser, Angela.

ANGELA. Well, believe me, they're always there.

TOM (*nods . . . only half pretending to disbelieve her*). Cops are leaning on you? (*She barely nods, turns away.*) When did *this* start?

ANGELA. About . . . three, four weeks.

TOM. You mean since I began coming around so much again?

ANGELA. I think so.

TOM. Well, that would be nice, if I'm makin' them nervous. But I have to say it, honey – there's no cruiser down there now.

ANGELA. You're . . . not leaving, are you?

TOM. I'll stay a few minutes, if you want. (*He removes his coat. She goes to the bed and sits. He sits in an armchair.*) Who's Leontine?

ANGELA. Leontine?

TOM. Yeah, you just went into her; she come after me like the wrath of God.

ANGELA. I never heard that name.

TOM. She's quite a broad.

ANGELA. Why – what'd she say?

TOM. Nothin' much. She sounds like a whore in a house. (*This seems to wilt her a little with yet another grief.*) You really don't remember *none* of it?

ANGELA (*pressing her temples apprehensively*). No. But listen . . . there is always a cruiser, Tom. (*He looks at her, silent.*) I'm telling you, they're down there all the time.

TOM (*he takes her hand*). I believe you.

ANGELA (*relief and gratitude on her face*). Even two of them sometimes . . .

TOM. Sit down. (*He puts her in a chair, sits opposite her and claps his hands together to inspire hope.*) I have a feeling tonight is going to break the ice.

ANGELA (*she is glad for their unity, and also digging in against it*). . . . . Just let me get my wind a little.

TOM. Good, get your wind. (*Feeling some semblance of control, he spreads out on the chair, chuckles . . .*) I never knew anybody where everytime I see her there's some big surprise – you're a soap opera. I keep waitin' for the next instalment.

ANGELA (*with tragic pride*). Yeah, well – I've had a life, kid.

TOM. Like now with these cruisers you keep seein'–

ANGELA. Not that I 'keep seeing', – they're *there*.

TOM. So what you're telling me is – it's the cops that've got you scared. Right?

She glances at him, loaded with other considerations.

You wouldn't want to give me a definite yes or no on that.

She turns to him, her gaze unreadable.

Okay, then it's yes.

ANGELA. Tom?

TOM. Uh huh?

ANGELA (*another message runs parallel with her words*). You're not realising the problem . . . (*Slight pause.*) I'm talking about *you*.

He was momentarily turned away from her; now he faces her. Slight pause.

TOM. What about me?

ANGELA (*cautiously*). You've got to start being more careful and watch every step you take . . .

TOM (*affects a grin, blushing with anger*). I hope I'm not hearing this right, Angela.

ANGELA (*with apology*). . . . I'm only telling you what I know. You should start being more . . .

TOM (*cutting her off*). – Honey, listen to me. I was a New York cop for twenty-four years; I been threatened by *experts*, so you can imagine that some Mack Sennett Police Department is not my idea of the Holy Terror, y'know? And I wish you would say this in case somebody should happen to ask you . . .

ANGELA (*trying to be testy*). . . . Nobody's asking me anything.

TOM (*seething*). But just in case they did, though – you tell them that I am on the Epstein case to the end of the bitter end . . .

ANGELA. . . . I'm not trying to . . .

TOM. . . . And there is nothing anybody can do about that, Angela – right?

ANGELA. That couldn't be better with me, Tom.

TOM. It wouldn't matter what it was with you, honey, or with anybody else. Get the picture?

ANGELA. You're one of a kind; honestly, Tom, you really stand tall. (*She comes to him, kisses him.*) Take me some place, let me make you happy again. Come on.

TOM (*holding both her hands*). Listen, never be the only one who knows something . . .

ANGELA (*looking contritely at the floor*). I know . . .

TOM. If somebody else knows it too, that's your best protection.

She nods agreement. He mimes playing pool.

The table's all set up, you want to start hittin' a few?

The moment of decision is on her, and she gives him a lost smile and turns away again.

I know you want to, Angie.

ANGELA (*a desperate little laugh*). You know? – Sometimes you talk just like Jimmy Cagney.

TOM (*sighs*). Oh, honey, are we gonna talk about Cagney now?

ANGELA. Well you do, you get that same sweet-and-sour thing. And the same brass balls.

TOM (*flattered despite himself*). Well, let's face it, Cagney was my god. (*Snaps his fingers, still seated he goes into a light little shuffling tap dance with a chuck of his head.*) 'Take me out to the ball game . . .'

ANGELA (*genuinely delighted, relieved*). Hey, wonderful!

TOM. Sure, and Pat O'Brien, Spencer Tracey . . . Christ, all those great Irishmen, tough and honest to a man. The moves in them days was Mick-Heaven. The only crooks were Italians.

ANGELA. You'd been great in a movie.

TOM. What as – the dumbest bookie on the block?

ANGELA. No, something dignified – like the first Irish Pope.

TOM. Jesus, you really like me, don't you.

ANGELA. I adore you, Tom. You've saved my life more than you'll ever know.

She draws him to her on the bed and snuggles onto his lap. He doesn't mind at all, and grins at her.

Do me once more.

TOM. No more, Ange, I'm sorry – it does something to my judgment.

ANGELA. I could make you fly around the room. You're my ideal, Tom.

TOM. Come on, kid.

ANGELA. You know, Father Paulini once said that if I'd known a man like you earlier in my life, I'd have turned out a completely different person. But once my father'd raped me, I always expected a man to go right for my ass.

TOM. Mmmm.

ANGELA (*slaps his cheek lightly*). Can't you get your mind off the case for *one minute* and just talk to me like a person?

TOM. It's after eleven p.m., Ange, I'm tired.

ANGELA. Know what I love? When you talk about being a cop in the old days in New York. Would you? – It soothes me. Talk about the Communion Breakfasts. (*She rests her head on his chest.*) And how important the Church was, right?

TOM (*sighs in boredom – although he likes it, too. He glances down at her, sensing his power . . .*). Oh yeah, the Church was really important in the Department in those days. Like any cop who took money from whores . . . or like dope money . . . the priest lay his head open.

ANGELA. Really? Even dope?

TOM. Sure . . . even the Mafia wouldn't touch dope in those days . . .

ANGELA (*incredulously*). Jesus.

TOM. It was a whole different world. (*Grins.*) Like one time they had me guarding the money in the Yankee Stadium office; great big piles of cash on the table. And I ask one of the officials – bein' that they were getting me for nothin', with the city payin' my salary, and all – if I could maybe get a hot dog sent up. So he says sure, gimme fifty cents, I'll send down. Imagine? – I'm watchin' half a million bucks for them and I couldn't even steal a free dog.

ANGELA. I can just see you there . . . with all that money . . . and nobody even giving you a dog. (*Her fear returns in a sweep and she is suddenly welling up.*) Oh, God, Tom . . .

TOM (*turning her face to him*). What is it, honey . . . come on, tell me! (*He hesitates before her vulnerability, then suddenly kisses her on the mouth.*)

ANGELA. Come on, Tom – please! Screw me, split me. I'll never forget that last time. You're a bull. Please! I want you!

He gets to his feet, disturbed by his unforseen kiss. She is sent into a real outpouring of sobbing – in mourning, as it were, for her wasted life which denied her a man like this . . . he tends to her, smoothing her hair.

TOM. Listen now – I could arrange protection. I could have you taken where it's safe. Just tell me what's got you so scared? (*She reaches for him again . . .*) I'd love to, honey, but I'm goddamned if I ever change this subject with you again. It's my professional reputation, my livelihood!

ANGELA (*even here there is a faint air of her improvising*). I'm going to die.

TOM. I hate hearing you say that.

ANGELA. I can't get air. (*Slight pause.*)

TOM. You been to confession?

ANGELA. Yes. But I . . . (*Breaks off.*)

TOM. You couldn't tell him about this, huh? (*She shakes her head.*) I wish I was smarter, kid; I wish I could say the right thing. You don't know how I hate to see you suffering like this.

ANGELA. You've been wonderful, Tom.

TOM. Why can't you give me a little faith? (*A silent struggle in her; she touches his face, then turns away.*) Why are these cops leaning on you, can you just tell me that?

ANGELA (*she is silent for a moment; some resolve seems to harden*). Tom.

TOM. I'm listening.

ANGELA. I want you to tell me one thing from the heart. – What's the single main thing you want from this case?

TOM (*uncomprehending*). The single . . . ?

ANGELA. Well is it to get Felix out on the street, or . . . ?

TOM. Well, no, I want the people who put him in there too.

ANGELA. Why? You want revenge or something?

TOM. There's such a thing as the administration of justice, honey – which in this county, is laying on the floor like a busted dozen eggs, it is a fucking farce. – But I don't think I understand the question.

ANGELA. . . . Nothing. I was just wondering what you wanted.

TOM. Fair enough, – I'll answer you! – Callaghan's got to be blasted out of the prosecutor's office for falsifying evidence, okay? And Bellanca and his whole crew of detectives for conspiring with him . . . (*Grinning.*) Now tell me why you asked a question like that?

ANGELA. Well, I agree with Bellanca . . .

TOM. Why? – Callaghan's worse; publicly calling me a 'ridiculous pseudo-detective' and trying to lift my license . . . but we're back in this tic-tac-toe again. Are you going to tell me why the cops are so heavy on you, or not? (*She moves as though framing an answer.*) And I beg you on bended knees, don't start wrappin' me in another ball of wool.

ANGELA (*looks down at her hands, almost patently evading*). The thing, y'see, is that I was so humiliated after what my father . . .

TOM. (*impatiently*). Darlin', I *know* your father raped you, but . . .

ANGELA. Oh, am I boring you?

TOM. I didn't say you . . .

ANGELA (*fish on the line, she swims away, half sobbing, half furious*). Well, I beg your fucking pardon!

TOM (*furiously*). Angela, I am just about convinced starting this minute that you are full of shit! I don't think you know a goddamned thing about this case and I am going home! Forever!

He picks up his coat; she grabs him.

ANGELA (*in great alarm*). Can't we talk for two minutes without the case . . . ?

TOM. I want an answer to what I asked you – what got you into this in the first place? Where are you comin' from, Angela, what is your connection!

ANGELA (*gripping her head*). I'm going crazy!

TOM. I'm turning into a laughing stock! I walk into the Burrington Court House the other day and I had a hard time not to put a fist through some of the stupid smiles on those cops standing around – they all know I'm still on this case after nearly four years . . .

ANGELA. Well, fuck' em!

TOM (*takes a beat – quietly*). Well, you're really chock full of solutions. I understand a very colourful description of me is goin' around the courthouses – I am the detective who couldn't track a diuretic elephant on a glacier.

ANGELA. A diuretic elephant . . . ? (*She breaks out laughing.*)

TOM (*grinning*). Gives you a vivid picture, doesn't it?

Their eyes meet and she sees the steel in his eyes and turns away.

All right, baby – take care of yourself. I guess tonight ends it between us, kid. And I may as well tell you straight – I am humiliated. (*He waits for her to start it going again; then . . .*) And I'm sorry for your sake; that you couldn't level with me; cause in my opinion, the reason you're sick is that you lie. (*He starts to leave, he sees her near paralysis of fear.*) It's okay. I've got a whole other way to move ahead. It would've been easier with you but I can make it alone. Take care, kid – I'm out of your life.

He crosses the room to the door, starts getting his arms into his raincoat – stalling, but not too obviously. She watches him in desperation. Her voice trembling, her anxiety pitched high . . .

ANGELA. Can you believe . . . ? (*She breaks off.*)

TOM (*alerted*). Believe what, dear?

ANGELA (*wringing her hands, struggling in fear of going on . . .*). That a man can be a fine and good man and still do something that's . . . just terrible?

TOM (*avid now*). Sure.

ANGELA. I mean a thing . . . that is not really in his nature to do, but that he has to because . . . it's all so . . . (*Almost crying out.*) . . . rotten in this place?

TOM (*more warmly now*). Absolutely. I believe that. If I thought life was straight lines I'd be workin' for the Highway Department. (*Slight pause.*) . . . Like who are you referring to?

She sends him a terrified glance; there is some longing in her look, too. Her breathing now becomes raspy and he helps her to the bed where she sits, gasping and glancing up at him half in terror and half in hope.

I always said you had class, darling, you know why? –

'Cause of your conscience; most people would just sign
out and butter their own potatoes, but not you. You suf-
fer.

His expectations high, he watches her regain her breathing,
but she doesn't venture any further.

Who were you talking about?

She glances at him, but nothing more.

Kid, now listen to me and hold on tight – I am six inches
from thinking that *you* were part of the frameup they laid
on Felix . . .

ANGELA (*furiously*). How can you be such a stupid son of a
bitch!

TOM. . . . And that you're still part of it right now, and trying
to keep me from finding out what went down! Which
would make you about the lowest cunt since Hitler! (*Push-*
ing up his coat collar.) Take care of yourself. This time it's
for good.

ANGELA (*with breathless veracity, and really trying* not *to break*
down in weeping). After five years you don't know the first
thing about this case.

TOM (*pause. He turns to her at the door*). . . . Jesus, the way
you say that goes right down to my haemorrhoids.

ANGELA. Believe me, darling . . . zee-ro. (*She holds up*
forefinger and thumb, touching.)

TOM. You telling me that Felix Epstein is guilty? (*Long*
pause.)

ANGELA. Felix is innocent. (*She heaves for breath; a real at-*
tack, she lies down.)

TOM (*goes to her quickly*). What should I do! You want a doctor?

She rises on one arm, gasping.

Tell me what to do!

She rocks back and forth; he bores in filled with aggressive
need.

All right, can you confirm one fact – did Callaghan fake the picture that nailed Felix? Or don't you know?

She screams, frightened of him.

– What are you doing? . . . Oh, no, Angela!

She presses her fists against her chest and her elbows against her sides with her shoulders pushed upward as though she were trying to become small, like a young child. He recognises this.

Don't do that – ! Please stop that, Angela!

He makes a move toward her.

ANGELA. Don't you touch me! (*She skitters into a corner, blindly staring at him.*)

TOM (*reaching toward her protectively*). Ange . . .

With a frightened scream, she cowers all scrunched up, terror in her face. A sound from her mouth, high and childlike.

Is it 'Emily'?

ANGELA. Don't, please . . . !

TOM. Okay, Emily . . . (*Opening his coat and holding out his palms.*) . . . see? Nothin' on me at all. Okay, darling? Why don't you come out and we get a little ice cream from the corner? Your father's gone, honey – honest, he won't be comin' back tonight.

He takes one step toward her but she reacts in fright so he backs up.

Okay, dear, you stay there and I'll just make a call, Okay? Take your time, have a little nap if you want. (*He goes and sits beside the phone, dials. As he waits, he playfully twiddles his fingers at her.*) Hya, darlin'. (*Into the phone.*) Sorry to bother you again, Mrs Levy . . . thanks a lot. (*To* ANGELA.) How about a chocolate fudge later? – I'm sorry, Josh, – No, no, I hate to bother you so late . . . – Oh, zonked out again, being Emily now, all scrunched up like an eight year old, it's pathetic. Listen, bad news . . . she claims it's the cops leaning on her. – I think it could be, yes. But she's been seeing two police cruisers parked on the block every night . . . but I looked and there's none down there, you see? But why do I still believe her? – Oh absolutely! I believe her, Josh! – Except if it was just that I invested so much in her I could walk away; wasting your time is most of what you do in this business. (*Listens, a rapt stare now.*) Now *that*'s funny; I was thinking of Maria all the way down in the car before, like she was sitting in the seat beside me. – There is a similarity, yes; the same kind of sexiness, maybe. (*Glances up at* ANGELA. *A shake of the head, wondrously.*) – So in other words, I've blown four and a half years . . . on a dream! (*Resistance hardens his face.*) Except, goddammit, Josh, she was the first one who told me about Carl Linstrom; – yes, the man who was seen covered with blood, running away from the Kaplan house. And now I have four separate witnesses to corroborate and I can't get the police to make an arrest! You see what I mean? – She knows too many facts for just a crazy, fantasising whore . . . ! (ANGELA *sits up, he sees her.*) . . . We're back on the air, I'll be in touch. (*He hangs up. She approaches him, staring.*) Well! What do you say, Bubbles – welcome back! (*She stares at him, puzzled, suspicious. He is defensive . . .*) I made a little call. (*Her stare is unrelenting.*) To my friend, the psychiatrist. Sends his regards. (*Her stare remains.*) I told you – he's my quarterback sometimes. He's still very interested in the case . . . You know, Felix being Jewish . . .

ANGELA. Some Jew! He didn't have the balls to join my committee.

TOM. Well, let's face it kid, neither did anybody else, that was a one-woman committee. (*He stands.*) Well, take care. I really got to hit the pike.

ANGELA. Wait, wait . . . we didn't even talk. What've you been working on lately?

TOM. Oh, nothing great.

ANGELA. Like what?

TOM. Corporation stuff mostly. Big ball bearing company; in fact – I've got to go out to Phoenix, investigate a guy they're about to make the vice president.

ANGELA. They still doing that shit?

TOM (*shrugs*). Well, you know – you can't have a homosexual vice president of a ball bearing company.

ANGELA. But how do you do that?

TOM. Ah, it's boring. I get his old airplane ticket stubs for the past few months; they usually travel on the company account; and see if he's been to some off-the-track town . . . you know, Ashtabula, Ohio; Grim City, Iowa; and I go to the gay bar and show the bartender his picture with a hundred dollar bill clipped to it, and he tells me if he's ever seen him there. I didn't used to mind it, but I don't like it anymore. But . . . (*He shrugs, with a sigh, rubbing two fingers together.*)

ANGELA. And for that he can't be vice president?

TOM. Well, they're scared of blackmail. And you know, he's supposed to be a good example.

ANGELA. To who?

TOM. Who the hell knows anymore? (*At the door.*)

ANGELA (*the same lostness and tension grip her but she no longer pleads for him to stay*). Would you take another look down the street before you go?

TOM. For you, I'll do it. (*He goes, opens the door, exits. She remains absolutely still, facing front. He returns.*) I don't see them.

ANGELA (*awakened*). Heh?

TOM. There's no cruiser down there.

ANGELA. Who?

TOM (*impatiently*). The cruiser! The cops you were so worried about.

ANGELA (*preoccupied*). Oh.

TOM. Oh! – Five minutes ago you were . . . Oh, forget it. I don't see Philly in the living-room. So why don't you try to relax now, Okay? – Maybe I'll see you sometime. (*She is lost in thought. He turns her face to him.*) . . . Ange?

ANGELA. I used to be with Charley.

TOM (*electrified*). . . . Callaghan?

She is silent.

Talking about the prosecutor?

ANGELA (*hard as a nail*). I will deny everything if you ever try to hurt him with it – I'm myself now, Tom, you understand what I'm saying to you? I will never hurt Charley. (*She takes a sudden inhale.*)

TOM (*stunned*). Okay. – Was this like one or two shots or . . . ?

ANGELA. Three, four times a week over two years. We went to Canada and Puerto Rico, couple of times.

TOM. And when did it end? (*Slight pause.*)

ANGELA. He's come back to me.

TOM. You seeing him *now*?

ANGELA (*a sudden expressiveness, closeness*). He's the love of my life, Tom.

TOM. Right. – This is quite a blow to my mind, darlin'. (*Slight pause.*) You mean like . . . you were exercising with him while he was prosecuting Felix?

ANGELA. Yes. (*Slight pause.*) – You don't believe me.

TOM (*slight pause*). – Well . . . it sure ties certain things together. That's the reason you came to the trial every day, is that it? – to buck him up?

ANGELA (*hesitation*). I wasn't there to buck him up. (*Slight pause.*) I was there taking notes – which you saw me do, and which you read.

TOM (*apologetically*). That's right, honey . . .

ANGELA. Some whores can take notes, y'know – I went to Mary Immaculate, which just happens to have the highest academic record in the state. I can also add, subtract and multiply . . .

TOM. Now, don't go off into a . . .

ANGELA (*deeply agitated*). Sometimes I don't understand why the fuck I talk to you at all, O'Toole. I mean, Jesus . . . (*He lets her find her calm as she walks about shaking her head.*) I may come off the street but that don't mean I've still got rocks in my head. I'm going to get out of this situation, you know.

TOM. I hope so, Angela. – Out of what situation?

ANGELA (*retreating*). Never mind. Just don't forget what I said about hurting Charley. I can murder you if you do that.

TOM. How you going to murder me, Ange?

ANGELA. Don't worry, I can do it.

TOM. We're gonna forget you said that, Okay?

ANGELA. I'm not threatening you!

TOM. The second time tonight . . .

ANGELA. I didn't mean that I . . .

TOM. Stop-right-here-Angela! Charley Callaghan has tried to get my Investigator's Licence lifted because I have gotten reversals on two of his biggest cases, just like I am going to do on this one . . .

ANGELA. I did not mean . . . !

TOM. . . . So you can ask me not to hurt Charley but please do not try to scare me with him because that is to laugh! Now what'd you want to say? – I mean I hope you are not conveying some kind of a threat from somebody.

ANGELA. You know? – Sometimes I think you ought to see a psychiatrist.

TOM. Oy gevalt! – Kid, you are going to end me up pluckin' chickens in the funny farm!

ANGELA. But you suspect everything I say! You tell me to trust you, but do you trust me?

TOM. Darlin', look – let's get back to taking those notes during the trial;.can I ask what they were for?

ANGELA. 'Cause I knew Felix had nothing to do with Kaplan's murder, and I wanted to prove it.

TOM. I'm still not getting the picture, dear, forgive me. You were in the hammock with Charley at nights and in the days taking notes to *dis*prove his case?

ANGELA. We broke up over the case.

TOM (*impressed*). Oh!

ANGELA. I couldn't stand what it was doing to him. He'd come back from the court and we'd go out to the beach and build a fire and he'd stare into it with tears pouring down his cheeks. Sometimes he would look up into the stars and try to pray. Charley studied for priesthood, you know . . .

TOM. I heard that.

ANGELA. He still does retreats.

TOM. Yeah, well . . . I guess I must've missed his spiritual side.

ANGELA. You have a closed mind: I'm telling you he's a whole other person than you believe.

TOM. Listen, I'm always ready to learn. – What were the tears for though?

ANGELA. . . . We even went to churches in San Juan.

TOM. Together?

ANGELA. Well, we sat in different parts . . .

TOM. In other words, the tears were that he was rigging the Epstein case, or what?

ANGELA *doesn't answer at once.*

Ange? Please. – What were the tears?

ANGELA. It wasn't his fault. The chief of detectives handed him the case, all tied with a ribbon and ready for trial . . .

TOM. Bellanca. (ANGELA *nods.*) So *Bellanca* faked the photograph? (*She nods again.*)

ANGELA. Charley didn't want to touch the case. They made him push it. I know how you hate him, Tom, but you have to believe me . . .

TOM. Tell me something – why did they pick on Felix in the first place? Why him?

ANGELA. Total accident – he just happened to have come to town to visit his uncle, Abe Kaplan; it's exactly like he claimed – he was trying to get Kaplan to take him into the accountancy firm.

TOM. But why did they have to go through that whole charade when they could have just gone out and picked up Linstrom? – They had to know Linstrom was covered with blood that night – they *had* the killer any time they wanted him.

ANGELA (*slight pause*). Because Linstrom was a runner.

TOM. A runner?

ANGELA. For Kaplan. (*Slight pause.*)

TOM. Abe Kaplan was in drugs?

ANGELA. In! – Abe *ran* the drugs in this town. – God, you are stupid. You're pathetic.

TOM (*embarrassed*). I knew Abe was the big loan shark . . .

ANGELA. That was the front.

TOM. . . . So they latched onto Felix . . . tell me again, will ya?

ANGELA (*impatiently*). To make it look like a family argument – the uncle and the nephew . . .

TOM. But Charley's the chief . . . (*She silently assents.*) . . . if he felt so bad about it, why did he have to go ahead and make the case against Felix?

ANGELA *is staring.*

Don't go out on me, will you? (*She stares. He bursts out.*) This is horrendous. – You cannot go out on me now! Why couldn't they arrest Linstrom?

ANGELA. Because it could open the whole can of worms.

TOM. What can is that, honey?

ANGELA (*this is deeper than she wanted to go. Barely audible*). The police connection.

TOM. To the drugs.

ANGELA. That's why they're parking down there.

He gives her an evasive nod.

They are, you know.

He gives her a deeper nod of assuagement. But his thought has moved to something else at which he stares now . . .

They are parking down there, Tom . . . (*She starts angrily for the door, but he forces her into an embrace.*)

TOM. If I was to ask you, Angela – how do you know Abe Kaplan was in drugs . . . can I ask you that?

ANGELA. *doesn't answer at once, moving away from him.*

. . . Because I'm trying to be as objective as I can, you see, dear? I mean let's face it, Abe was one of the pillars, right? With the synagogue and the Boys Town and you name it, and a lot of people are going to find that hard to believe, you know?

ANGELA (*decides, faces him*). I used to be with Abe.

TOM (*rocked*). . . . . No kiddin', *Abe*?

ANGELA. A lot. We went down to Bimini together.

TOM. Bimini.

ANGELA. Twenty, twenty-five times.

TOM. Isn't Bimini one of the . . . ?

ANGELA. I carried for him coming back. I would deliver the stuff to Bellanca.

A long pause. He moves now, facing front.

That's why I'm so upset with them parking down there, you see?

TOM (*he sets his jaw*). But they are not parking down there, honey.

ANGELA (*springing up, gripping her head*). They are parking

down there!!
He shuts his eyes.
And you . . . you've got to start taking precautions.

TOM. We must be on some kind of wave length together . . .
(*He takes a snubnose revolver out of his pocket.*) I never carry
this, but I'm leaving the house tonight and, for some
reason . . . I stuck it in my pocket before going out the
door. (*He puts the gun away.*) Incidentally, if Bellanca's
holding any kind of . . . like a drug rap over you, the best
thing you could do is level with me, you know; the Feds
would protect a witness against drug dealers, they have a
witness-protection programme and it's serious . . . You're
not going out on me, are you?

ANGELA. – No, I'm here. (*Her voice breaks in the tension and
she moves, holding down a sobbing fit.*)

TOM. How long can you go on with this tension? You're
going to explode.
She simply shakes her head.
Has anybody said exactly what they want from you? – Is
it to get me to stop coming around? – or what?

ANGELA (*staring ahead, almost stupidly*). For me to give him
his letters back.

TOM (*this is new . . . he uses a fine degree of charm*). . . . Which
letters we talkin' about?
She stares.
Charley wrote you letters?
She turns to him blankly.
About your relationship, or what?

ANGELA. About his struggle.

TOM. Like with his conscience.
She is staring ahead.
– He wrote you a letter about it?

ANGELA (*nodding*). Nine.

TOM. No kiddin' – (*With the faintest tinge of doubt now.*) – nine letters?

ANGELA (*reaches for his hand*). Don't leave me, Tom.

TOM. I'm with you, Ange. And where are they – these letters?

ANGELA. . . . I have them some place.

TOM. Oh.

ANGELA. I always had to have candles for him in the apartment.

TOM. Candles.

ANGELA. It helped him – to look into flames. I was the closest to him, closer than his wife. He couldn't keep it to himself anymore. I begged him. I prayed for him but he had to push the case, or he'd lose everything. I told him, I said, 'You could be anything, you could be President of the United States! – Don't do this to an innocent man, God will take it out of your flesh!' – I thought if he saw me in court taking notes he'd realise that I meant business and I would not let Felix rot in jail . . . and it would make him stop the case. (*She breathes in suddenly, deeply, and the eyes seem to be going blind.*)

TOM. Don't leave me, Angela.

ANGELA (*gripping his hand*). I'm staying. I'm trying . . . Oh, God, Tom, you don't know, you don't know . . .

TOM. Tell me, what, what?

ANGELA. . . . They picked me up off the street today. (*She is in open terror.*)

TOM. Cops?

ANGELA. I lied to you before . . . When I was walking past Ramsey's piano store, they suddenly came up beside me and jammed me into the cruiser, and drove me around, two cops and a detective. Caught my hair in the goddamned door!

TOM. Bastards! – What'd they want?

ANGELA. That if I didn't straighten up I'd be floating in the bay. (*She weeps. He holds her in his arms.*)

TOM (*he turns to the door*). So they're leaning on you for the letters, is that bottom line?

ANGELA *nods*.

Why don't you give them to them?

ANGELA. But I'd never see him again.

TOM. You honest to God see him now?

ANGELA. He comes, once or twice a week. But now it's only to get them back.

TOM. You're not making it with him anymore.

ANGELA. Only once in a while. (*Now she curls up on the bed.*)

TOM. Can I see the letters? (*She doesn't react.*) You want to go somewhere? My valise is in the car. (*She stretches a hand to him, tempted, conflicted.*) Get your coat on, come on, we'll ride somewhere and talk more. (*He holds her hand.*)

ANGELA. I'll die before I hurt him, Tom.

TOM. All right – Suppose you don't show me anything, just read me the relevant parts – you keep them in your hands. – Go on, get them.

She is in a fever of indecision. She gets off the bed, one moment covering her eyes with her hands, the next glancing at him as though trying to judge him. She opens a drawer off the dressing-table; hesitates, then takes out a brush and brushes her hair.

Darlin', listen to me – with that kind of evidence, I can put Felix back on the street by noon tomorrow.

ANGELA (*pressed*). I said I can't hurt Charley!

TOM (*furiously.*) Then why've you told me this?

ANGELA. I can't give you them now.

TOM. When then?

ANGELA. When I can!

He watches her for a long moment.

TOM. Angela – explain to me – why'd you tell me all this?

ANGELA. So you'd help me!

TOM. Help you how?

She looks directly into his eyes in an open appeal.

Are you telling me to drop Felix? You're not telling me that, are you?

She is silent.

Honey – you mean I just drive home now and go to sleep?

She is silent – furiously.

Talk to me.

ANGELA (*scared of him now*). I don't owe Felix Epstein – I fought for him!

TOM. How! You had a cannon and you threw some beanbags! And for five whole years you cold-bloodedly watched me chasing up one deadend after another and never said boo about this?

ANGELA. You never trusted a word I said, did you? Do you trust me even now? You know you don't!

TOM. What other man in your life ever believed in you like I did! How dare you say that to me! I'm damn near a laughing stock for believing in you. – Now give it to me straight – did you call me here tonight to get me to quit this case?

The load on her is crushing . . .

ANGELA. Ssssh! – Don't talk so loud . . .

TOM(*to the door*). Fuck Philly and fuck them!

The violence in the air sends her into quicker movements seeking escape and air . . .

Where are you comin' from, Angela, whose side are you on? What is happening here? (*With a cry in his voice, he grips her.*) Are they running you? Do they make you keep calling me?

ANGELA (*violently breaking from him, shaking a finger at him*). You know . . . you know . . . (*Groping breathlessly, she becomes rigidly straight; a new personality, a terribly austere, dignified lady with upper-class speech.*) . . . it might just be a terribly good idea for you to think a little more highly of me and stop irritating me!

TOM. Who's this now?

ANGELA. You are irritating me!

TOM. I refuse to talk to Renata!

ANGELA. Stop irritating me!

TOM (*even though knowing she is hardly able to hear him – in fact, she is softly hooting to herself as he speaks in order to block off his sounds and mock him*). Irritating *you*! You knew all these years where the bodies were buried and I'm irritating you? You're lucky I quit the booze, your face'd be running down that wall by now! (*Swelling, pulling up his pants.*) The enormity!

ANGELA. Enormity? (*She bursts out laughing rather merrily.*)

TOM. And what if I don't quit? Would that . . . put you in some kind of an emergency?

ANGELA (*as though quite beyond all harm*). Me!

TOM. . . . In other words, sweetie . . . are you trying to tell me that we're not really all that great friends? – Is that it?

ANGELA (*confused, but adopting an indignant stance*). Now you listen . . . !

TOM. You listen to me – this is still the United States of America, you don't have to lay down in front of those punks.

ANGELA. Well, I must say . . . what astounds *me* is how you get to think *you're* such a high grade cultured individual and such a great Catholic . . . !

TOM. All right, Renata, come! I'll find a doctor for you in · Boston.

ANGELA. . . . But all you really are is gutteral!

TOM. Will you just blow that out your ass and talk straight?

ANGELA. . . . You can't help it, your whole manner is gutteral because your whole background is gutteral.

TOM. You're not even using the word right.

ANGELA. I mean who do you imagine you fuckin' are – just

because you read some magazines without any pictures?

TOM (*eyes rolling upward*). Jesus Christ . . .

ANGELA. *You* have the audacious contempt to call the Lord's name in vain?

TOM (*defeated*). Okay, Renata, let's just forget the whole . . .

ANGELA. *You* can call me Miss Marshall. Stupid bastard.

TOM (*laughs, despite everything*). By this time Miss Renata Marshall ought to know that a respectable lady like her doesn't call people stupid bastards.

ANGELA. Which I would be delighted to do if these stupid bastards had the mental competence to understand any other kind of language, you dumb shit.

TOM. Touché. (*He spreads his arms out.*) Okay, pull out the nails. I want to come down. I'm through, hon . . . for tonight. But I'll be back and we can start *all over again!*
She is surprised, frightened too as the air goes out of her.
(*In a mixture of laughter and fury . . .*)
That's right, Baby. (*Partly toward the door.*) I will never give up until Felix Epstein is walking the street! Plus lover-boy Callaghan gets a long number across the back of his shirt – if, in fact, you ever really laid him at all outside of your mental waterbed!

ANGELA (*exhausted, she starts to droop*). Well, you don't say . . .

TOM. Then where's his letters? Show me one single proof that this is not another one of your spitball delusions?

ANGELA. *My* delusions! *My* delusions! And what about your delusions? All of a sudden *I'm in the United States of America*? (*Tears are pouring into her eyes.*) And *I've* got *delusions*? This town is in the United States? This police force . . . ?

TOM (*his pain surges and he protectively embraces her, chastened*). I gotcha, honey.

ANGELA (*weeping*). Help me – for Christ's sake, Tom!

TOM. Sssh! (*He cuts off her weeping by kissing her mouth and holds her against himself with great force. And turning her face up . . .*) Did you really think you could get me off the case?

ANGELA (*covers her face and sobs in defeat*). My God!

The phone rings: they are both caught off guard. She goes and picks up the phone with high tension, her voice fearful, very faint – clearly, she has some specific caller in mind. Yes? (*Surprised and pleased – charm suddenly warms her voice.*) Oh! – Oh, I'm so sorry, I forgot all about it! (*A near stutter.*) Well . . . well . . . well, yes, sure . . . (*She looks confused at her watch but can't quite focus on it . . . and with a glance at Tom, sotto voce.*) What's the time?

TOM (*sotto voce*). Ten to twelve.

ANGELA (*with a warmly thankful glance at him*). Sure, I can make it, I have have to get dre . . . (*But glancing down at herself, she breaks off.*) . . . in fact, I am dressed already . . . (*Feels her hair, surprised that it is in place.*) . . . in fact, my hair's practically done . . . Ah . . . (*Ineffectually shielding the phone – oddly – with a half-turn away from Tom.*) . . . where is it again? Oh, right! (*Nearly whispering.*) And what's the room? Okay. (*Smiles.*) . . . You too, pussycat! (*She hangs up. She has expanded with a new pleasure-shame, an identity that is palpable. She turns to face him.*) I had an appointment I forgot all about.

TOM. You did? How come?

ANGELA. I don't know, I just blew it.

TOM. They say that means a person really doesn't want to go.

ANGELA. You got time to drop me?

TOM (*this is more difficult*) . . . Where's that?

ANGELA (*evasively*). Well . . . like the corner of Main and Benson would be okay.

TOM (*an instant – he looks at her almost incredulous, then turns away, and with dry rage, humiliation*). Come on.

ANGELA (*with fresh energy*). Just got to fix my face, be right with you. Put your feet up. (*She turns to go up to the bathroom.*)

TOM (*with an open resentment*). Why don't I drop you right at the hotel instead of on the street – it's only a few more yards? (*She turns back to him, ashamed – as it were – for his sake.*)

ANGELA. . . . The corner would be okay.

He doesn't reply, his head turned angrily away from her, although he is attempting to grin. She breaks the moment, hurries into the bathroom . . . another moment . . . and in a dispirited way he picks up the phone and dials. He waits, greatly tired, an inward look in his deadened face.

TOM. This could be tapped, you want to hang up? – Good, turn it on. You rolling? (*As for a record.*) Abe Kaplan was hit by one of his own crazy runners. – That's correct, he was into drugs, Josh . . . with the detective squad. – Why is it incredible? – Because she was Abe's broad. And Callaghan's too, incidentally. (*He listens.*) Look, talk to you later, I just wanted to tell you this much before I go outside. – No don't worry. I'll be all right – What do you want me to do, call the police? – Well, that's nice of you to offer, but she's only going to twist you around too, isn't she? I mean I've got to stop looking for some red tag that says 'Real' on it; I don't have the education, but I have the feeling and I'm just going to have to follow my nose, wherever it takes me, y'know? – If it's real for me then that's the last question I can ask, right? – Well, I'm not sure yet, but somehow I think I can decide pretty quick now, maybe tonight. – I do, yes . . . I feel kind of relieved now that I've thought of this. And at the same time like in a fog on top of a mountain where the next step is either six inches down or five thousand feet. (*A laugh.*) – It *is* a mystery, but I still have my ignoramus opinion, Josh; I think that somewhere way upstream the corruption is poisoning the water and making us all a little crazy. – Her? No, she's feeling great now! In the toilet getting saddled up for some honcho in the Hilton, and ten minutes ago rasping out her last and final breath! (*He laughs.*) – No, kid, it's not unreal, it's just horrendous!

ANGELA *enters.*

And here she comes now, riding on her elephant, our Lady of the Hilton, looking like seven million bucks!

She laughs delightedly.

You hear her? She's laughing, fulla beans.

ANGELA (*calls into phone*). Hya, Doc!

TOM. Now if only Felix could get the joke – Right, talk to you soon. (*He hangs up.*)

ANGELA. Before we go down – if those cops give me any trouble, we're going to midnight mass at St Jude's, Okay?

He laughs brazenly.

What are you laughing at?

TOM. What cops?

ANGELA (*gesturing toward door*). In the cruiser downstairs.

TOM (*totally loose and lost, he laughs*). What cruiser downstairs?

She looks shaken, distraught.

You stole five years of my life, you goddamn lunatic! I ought to wrap you around a lamp post.

ANGELA (*gathering herself in protest*). But there's always one there!

TOM (*mimicking*). There's always one there! (*Clenching his fists to keep them off her.*) How did you get into my life!!

With a look of apprehensive uncertainty mixed with indignation, she turns and dashes out the door. He strides about, full of self-hatred.

How did I get into this goddamn dream! My brain died! She murdered my brain . . . !

She enters, rather slowly, glancing at him with a new air of mock indignation. He reads this look, and takes an uncertain few steps toward the door, then halts and turns back to see her looking at herself in her hand mirror with bland assurance. He rushes out the door. She stares front. He re-enters.

ANGELA. Who's crazy now?

TOM. Angela . . . Christ, I'm sorry. Forgive me, will you?

She gives him a peeved look. Approaching her, arms extended . . .

Oh, Darlin' . . . Oh, Ange . . . I can't help it, I love you! (*He starts to embrace her but she frees herself.*)

ANGELA. Hey, watch the hair, for Christ sake! I'm serious, you've got to get yourself some help!

TOM (*apologetically*). But, honey, they weren't down there a little while ago . . .

ANGELA. Well, don't cops take leaks?

TOM (*anxious to forestall*). Look . . . what do you say we go and get a ravioli and a nice bottle of wine . . . ?

ANGELA (*imperatively*). *I have to go!*

TOM (*surprising himself, a cry*). *Why!* They don't have to run *every thing* in this world! . . . Listen . . . get in my car. Let me take you to Judge McGuire's house – you remember, he and I are close; he'll arrange federal protection; we can bust this case and you can . . . you can start a whole new life, darling. (*She stares into his face.*) And who knows, maybe we could still walk off into that sunset together? (*Taking her hand.*)

ANGELA. I can't.

TOM. Yes you could, if you believed in me.

ANGELA. No, not only you, Tommy, – I think you got me too late; all that went by. Come on, I'm late. (*She takes her coat off a chair, she starts upstage. He rushes to intercept her.*

TOM. Wait! I want to tell you something Dr Levy told me.

ANGELA. Levy! Levy's gutless.

TOM. He said I haven't been in love since I was twenty-five, so you like woke me from the dead, sexually, so . . .

ANGELA. Did he really say that?

TOM. So I handed you almost magical powers, like you could see in the dark through a slab of concrete.

ANGELA. Oh, Tommy . . .

TOM. . . . But I see now that whatever you know you're never going to tell me, because you don't want me off and away. That's it, isn't it – never, never, never.

ANGELA. Listen! – maybe if we could meet for a good long lunch tomorrow . . .

TOM. No more lunches!

ANGELA. Give me one more chance to try to tell you, Tommy; that makes me happier than anything I've ever heard in my life – that I woke you from the dead. How about Pinnochio's, one o'clock?

TOM. No! Come, I'll drop you. I've got a man in jail. I've wasted too much time. (*He gets his coat and hat.*)

ANGELA. So this is it, then?

TOM. This has to be the last long night, yes. But you get evidence, something I can take into court, call me anytime – I just have to get to work, Okay?

ANGELA. Okay. Then I should tell you something to keep in mind. There's a whole side of this case you never even heard of. (*He goes stock still.*) Don't believe it, I don't care – but I have to tell you. You're not just leaving a crazy woman, you're leaving the case. 'Cause I'm the only one alive who knows. There are names that'd knock your head off, all the way to Boston, Washington, Providence and New York. The whole criminal justice system could be picked up by the tail like a dead rat. All you got now is the tip of the tip of the iceberg. – Good Luck. (*She opens the door and glances back.*) You still dropping me or is that out too? (*She sees him wipe a tear from his eye.*) What're you doing? (*She comes to him, incredulously.*) Why are you crying?

TOM (*shrugs, shakes his head*). . . . I guess because I still believe you.

ANGELA (*she draws his face to her and holds him*). I'll be at the corner table at the end of the bar.

TOM. NO!

ANGELA. Please come! (*She lowers her hands.*) Please come! It's all in me, Tom. And you're the only one who can ever get it out. I want to talk . . . quietly and . . . honestly. (*She is staring ahead.*) And then maybe it'll all be there . . . all the rottenness; and then it'll drop away. And then, maybe I could start to change my life. I'm going to expect you. You might just be amazed! (*She goes out. From the next room . . .*) Philly? Where are you? I'll be back in a couple of hours! (*Calling.*) Tom? Are you coming?

TOM (*eyes lifted*). Sorry, Felix . . . but hold on, don't let go, baby!

ANGELA (*from further off, calling*). What are you doing, you're making me late!

TOM (*shutting his eyes*). Dear God . . . make it only one more time!

ANGELA. Tom!

TOM. Yes! Coming, coming, coming . . . (*Hurrying out as the scene quickly blacks out.*)

Afterword

Two Way Mirror consists of two complementary plays which question the nature of the real. One, powerful and even melodramatic, examines the problem of recovering truth in a world marked by personal and social psychosis; the other, elegiac in tone, exists in the border territory marked out by memory and desire. Taken together with his extraordinary study of the theatrical content of private and public experience – *The Archbishop's Ceiling* – these plays mark a new phase in the career of America's leading dramatist.

Some Kind of Love Story is, on the face of it, a detective story but, like John Fowles' *The Enigma,* it is simultaneously a parody of the genre. The model of a concealed truth slowly exposed by rational process defers to an account of the problematic nature of reality and the complex motives of those who imagine themselves to be concerned to recover it.

Tom O'Toole is a detective, apparently anxious to solve a five year old murder. The key to the crime is Angela, a call girl whose clients, it seems, include both the criminal world and the public officials with whom she alleges they have colluded. But Angela is unstable to the extent that her personality is in constant danger of fragmenting. Profoundly frightened, she retreats into a series of alternative personalities. Manoeuvred into an emotional corner she opts for catatonia or offers only fragments of information, hints of further revelations. She promises evidence but offers none. The effect on the detective is wholly destabilising. If her accusations are true and those who investigated, charged and prosecuted the crime are the real guilty parties then moral distinctions begin to blur. He has to assess the credibility of a woman whose personality is disintegrating in front of him, in a world whose values seem no more than a convenient fiction. And there is a further complication in so far as the detective and would-be informant seem once to have been lovers. Since their justification for meeting is his investigation of the crime, what is it that maintains his interest? Is it, in short, a love story or a detective story? So long as she refuses to reveal the whole truth, assuming her to possess it, he continues to visit her. In that sense both perhaps have a vested interest in the game which they play, a game in which truth is pursued on the understanding that it must never be discovered. And with corruption apparently at the heart of things how can the real be recovered and a system of meaning maintained? As Tom O'Toole remarks, 'I've got to stop looking for some red tag that says 'Real' on it . . . I think that somewhere way upstream the corruption is poisoning the water and making us a little crazy. All that remains, it seems, is a plausible fiction. As he says, 'If it's real for me then that's the last question I can ask'. That, of course, leaves us with no agreed fictions let alone realities; not even, perhaps, the supposedly irreducible authenticity of a shared relationship. But this is only some kind of love story, a partial truth at best. The real thing seems beyond recovery. And yet, the murder itself was real enough and, if the detective is right, an innocent man is incarcerated. Perhaps, after all, his dogged determination is just what it appears to be even if his desire for justice leads him to wrestle with phantoms which make him doubt his own motives no less than the possibility of tracing truth to its lair.

Some years ago Arthur Miller found himself involved in a local criminal case. He intervened to secure the release of a man falsely accused of murder, in doing so exposing the public officials who had secured ther indictment. The ex-

perience plainly lies behind this play. The fascination, however, lies in the extent to which what, earlier in his career,
might have been recast as social drama is now forged into a
metaphysical work of great subtlety. And what appears as
melodrama is in effect a highly self-conscious study of a dis-
locating sensibility, a hunt for meaning and security con-
ducted on the very borders of madness by those who can
scarcely understand their own motives let alone press the
question of truth and reality to the point at which it may de-
stroy them both.

Its companion piece – *Elegy for a Lady* – is in a different
mood but is no less disturbing. It, too, seems to dissolve the
very characters which it presents. Starting with the simplest
of dramatic gestures – a figure alone in a darkened stage –
it creates character, plot and language only to make them
problematic, only to negate such meaning as has begun to
coalesce.

A man enters a boutique, tentatively, apparently seeking
a present for a dying woman. The proprietress responds,
slowly exposing, or so it seems, something of the man's relationship with the absent woman. In the course of the play,
however, an act of transference seems to occur as the proprietress is invested with some of the characteristics of that
woman. But in this play there are few if any certainties. It
begins, indeed, with the man alone, in a single beam of light,
staring, we are told, deep into himself. Slowly the light rises
and the details of the set become apparent, fragmentary,
barely sketched in, suspended in space. It is almost as though
it were being summoned into being by his mind, or, indeed,
as if he were a product of the proprietress's mind as she also
appears, motionless, in passive thought. She may or may not
be the dying woman and this her final fantasy; she may or
may not exist. At the end of the play the light fades, the man
remains for a moment and then he, too, disappears from the

stage.

It is tempting to see this as a play about the process of artistic invention since the characters and their setting are themselves, of course, summoned into being by the writer who sits at his or her desk in passive thought. But then perhaps it is concerned with memory or that world which is the product of need or hope. Or maybe it is an elegy for more than a single woman, lamenting and celebrating a life which begins with darkness and returns to it. But, like Beckett's or Pinter's work (and plays like *Krapp's Last Tape* and *Monologue* come to mind), it is best not decoded in terms of single meanings. It is a chimerical work, deceptively simple in its language and effects; a threnody for the self which creates but which is itself inevitably decreated by the pressure of time or the sheer fragility of its own inventions.

Two-Way Mirror, as its composite title suggests, contemplates the deceptive nature of the world in which its characters exist. At times they suspect a hidden world of meaning and coherence but when they look they see nothing but their own anxieties and desires reflected back at them. Like the figures in Plato's cave they see only shadows which they must take for reality until the chains which bind them are loosed. Miller no longer believes that reality to be as easily claimed or readily defined as once he did. But the need to do so remains – a phantom, a lure, an illusion, but, in some critical and inescapable sense, a necessity.

CHRISTOPHER BIGSBY

Methuen Modern Plays

include work by

Jean Anouilh
John Arden
Margaretta D'Arcy
Brendan Behan
Edward Bond
Bertolt Brecht
Howard Brenton
Mikhail Bulgakov
Noel Coward
Shelagh Delaney
David Edgar
Michael Frayn
Max Frisch
Jean Giraudoux
Simon Gray
Peter Handke
Vaclav Havel
Kaufman & Hart
Barrie Keeffe
Arthur Kopit
John McGrath
David Mercer
Arthur Miller
Mtwa, Ngema & Simon
Peter Nichols
Joe Orton
Harold Pinter
Luigi Pirandello
Stephen Poliakoff
David Rudkin
Jean-Paul Sartre
Wole Soyinka
C.P. Taylor
Peter Whelan
Nigel Williams

Methuen's Theatrescripts

SAMBA
by Michael Abbensetts
EAST-WEST & IS UNCLE JACK
  A CONFORMIST?
by Andrey Amalrik
BURIED INSIDE EXTRA
by Thomas Babe
DEREK & Choruses from AFTER
THE ASSASSINATIONS
by Edward Bond
SORE THROATS & SONNETS
  OF LOVE AND
  OPPOSITION
THE GENIUS
by Howard Brenton
THIRTEENTH NIGHT & A
  SHORT SHARP SHOCK!
by Howard Brenton (A Short Sharp
  Shock! written with Tony Howard)
SLEEPING POLICEMEN
by Howard Brenton and Tunde Ikoli
MOLIÈRE
by Mikhail Bulgakov (in a version by
  Dusty Hughes)
MONEY
by Edward Bulwer-Lytton
THE SEAGULL
by Anton Chekov (in a version by
  Thomas Kilroy)
TOP GIRLS
FEN
SOFTCOPS
by Caryl Churchill
SHONA, LUNCH GIRLS, THE
  SHELTER
by Tony Craze, Ron Hart, Johnnie
  Quarrell
POOR TOM & TINA
by David Cregan
WRECKERS
TEENDREAMS
MAYDAYS
by David Edgar
MASTERPIECES
by Sarah Daniels
THE BODY
by Nick Darke
OUR FRIENDS IN THE NORTH
by Peter Flannery
OTHER WORLDS
by Robert Holman
PEER GYNT
by Henrik Ibsen (translated by
  David Rudkin)
INSIGNIFICANCE
by Terry Johnson
FROZEN ASSETS
SUS

BASTARD ANGEL
by Barrie Keeffe
NOT QUITE JERUSALEM
by Paul Kember
BORDERLINE
by Hanif Kureishi
SERGEANT OLA AND HIS
  FOLLOWERS
by David Lan
TOUCHED
TIBETAN INROADS
THE RAGGED TROUSERED
  PHILANTHROPISTS
by Stephen Lowe
LAVENDER BLUE & NOLI
  ME TANGERE
by John Mackendrick
AMERICAN BUFFALO, SEXUAL
  PERVERSITY IN CHICAGO &
  DUCK VARIATIONS
by David Mamet
THICK AS THIEVES
WELCOME HOME, RASPBERRY,
  THE LUCKY ONES
by Tony Marchant
A NEW WAY TO PAY OLD
  DEBTS
by Philip Massinger
NICE, RUM AN' COCA COLA &
  WELCOME HOME JACKO
PLAY MAS, INDEPENDENCE &
  MEETINGS
by Mustapha Matura
LUNATIC AND LOVER
by Michael Meyer
OPERATION BAD APPLE
by G.F. Newman
SALONIKA
by Louise Page
STRAWBERRY FIELDS
SHOUT ACROSS THE RIVER
AMERICAN DAYS
THE SUMMER PARTY
FAVOURITE NIGHTS &
  CAUGHT ON A TRAIN
RUNNERS & SOFT TARGETS
by Stephen Poliakoff
BRIMSTONE AND TREACLE
by Dennis Potter
THE TIME OF YOUR LIFE
by William Saroyan
MY DINNER WITH ANDRÉ &
  MARIE AND BRUCE
by Wallace Shawn (My Dinner with
  André written with André
  Gregory)
LIVE THEATRE: Four Plays for
  Young People
by C.P. Taylor

BAZAAR & RUMMAGE,
GROPING FOR WORDS *and*
WOMBERANG
by Sue Townsend
THE ACCRINGTON PALS
CLAY
by Peter Whelan
RENTS
LENT
by David Wilcox
SUGAR AND SPICE & TRIAL
  RUN

W.C.P.C.
by Nigel Williams
THE GRASS WIDOW
by Snoo Wilson
HAS 'WASHINGTON' LEGS &
  DINGO
by Charles Wood
THE NINE NIGHT &
  RITUAL BY WATER
by Edgar White
CUSTOM OF THE COUNTRY
by Nicholas Wright

If you would like to receive, free of charge, regular information about new plays and theatre books from Methuen, please send your name and address to:

The Marketing Department (Drama)
Methuen London Ltd
North Way
Andover
Hampshire SP10 5BE